LIFE IN THE FINANCIAL MARKETS

LIFE IN THE FINANCIAL MARKETS

How they really work and why they matter to you

Daniel Lacalle

This work, originally published in Spanish, has been translated by Mark Lodge

WILEY

This edition first published 2015
© 2015 John Wiley & Sons, Ltd

Translated and updated from the Spanish edition *Nosotros, Los Mercados* published in 2013 by Ediciones Deusto, an imprint of Centro de Libros Papf, S.L.U.

Registered office
John Wiley & Sons Ltd, The Atrium, Southern Gate, Chichester, West Sussex, PO19 8SQ, United Kingdom

For details of our global editorial offices, for customer services and for information about how to apply for permission to reuse the copyright material in this book please see our website at www.wiley.com.

Wiley publishes in a variety of print and electronic formats and by print-on-demand. Some material included with standard print versions of this book may not be included in e-books or in print-on-demand. If this book refers to media such as a CD or DVD that is not included in the version you purchased, you may download this material at http://booksupport.wiley.com. For more information about Wiley products, visit www.wiley.com.

Designations used by companies to distinguish their products are often claimed as trademarks. All brand names and product names used in this book are trade names, service marks, trademarks or registered trademarks of their respective owners. The publisher is not associated with any product or vendor mentioned in this book.

Limit of Liability/Disclaimer of Warranty: While the publisher and author have used their best efforts in preparing this book, they make no representations or warranties with respect to the accuracy or completeness of the contents of this book and specifically disclaim any implied warranties of merchantability or fitness for a particular purpose. It is sold on the understanding that the publisher is not engaged in rendering professional services and neither the publisher nor the author shall be liable for damages arising herefrom. If professional advice or other expert assistance is required, the services of a competent professional should be sought.

Library of Congress Cataloging-in-Publication Data is available

A catalogue record for this book is available from the British Library.

ISBN 978-1-118-91487-8 (hbk)   ISBN 978-1-118-91496-0 (ebk)
ISBN 978-1-118-91495-3 (ebk)   ISBN 978-1-118-91494-6 (ebk)

Cover Design: Wiley
Cover Illustration: TK

Set in 11/15pt in ITC Garamond Std by Laserwords Private Limited, Chennai, India
Printed in Great Britain by TJ International Ltd, Padstow, Cornwall, UK

To my sons, Jaime, Daniel and Pablo, who are my pride and joy and the best thing that ever happened to me.

To Patricia, my love.

To my parents, Ángela and José Daniel, who raised me to think independently.

To my grandfather, who taught me to believe in myself.

Contents

Preface

In this book, I begin by trying to show the human side of the markets and the day-to-day joys and difficulties that they produce. Then I offer my general take on the economy and its crises and, lastly, provide a technical analysis of investing in the stock market based on my experiences as an investor.

It has been an immense pleasure for me to draw together several years of ideas, observations and analysis in a work that I hope the reader will find enlightening and to their liking.

By the time you have finished reading this book, the financial environment will have completely changed, the economy will be continuing to evolve and, with any luck, we will have the opportunity to continue learning something new. Remember that crisis is opportunity – as long as you also have a fair bit of luck.

Acknowledgements

Special thanks to:

Antonio González-Adalid, Emilio Ontiveros, Ken Griffin and Bernard Lambilliotte for everything I have learnt from them.

Roger Domingo, my editor Thomas Hyrkiel, Wiley, and Ediciones Deusto (Grupo Planeta), for their support.

Lorenzo Gianninoni, my first reader, for his invaluable feedback.

PART I

THE FINANCIAL MARKETS: WHO THEY ARE, WHAT THEY ARE, HOW THEY WORK

$$\boxed{\text{CHAPTER ONE}}$$

"THINKING AGAINST THE BOX"

We'd be delighted to make you an offer.

Liverpool Street, London, winter of 2005. They called me on a Thursday morning at my desk in an investment bank: "Daniel, I've spoken to my associates, and they'd like you to come over to meet them and have a chat with some of the team." The voice at the other end of the line was Toby, a client and friend who was managing $1 billion for one of the world's biggest hedge funds.[1]

"Of course, no problem," I replied, both intrigued and excited. "When?"

"You have a reservation on the eight o'clock flight. So you'll arrive here tomorrow morning and you can make the most of the day," Toby said. "We'll grab something to eat if you have enough time. Good luck."

---

[1] These funds, also called "alternative investment funds", aim to achieve completely positive instead of relative returns on an investment. To this end, they use various hedging instruments, which we will examine later.

"If I have enough time?" I wondered. What does he mean by that? "Good luck?" Well…

I told my wife, gave the bank an excuse for taking the day off on the Friday, packed my bag and headed for Heathrow.

The flight wasn't bad. I'm lucky enough to be able to sleep anywhere, and I wasn't expecting too much from the interviews, so I watched an inflight movie called *Lord of War*, by Andrew Niccol and starring Nicolas Cage. I read a bit of Steven Levitt's *Freakonomics*. And I went to sleep.

A car was waiting at the airport to take me to the offices.

The building was impressive. A huge glass tower, in which the investment fund occupied four floors: one allotted to meeting rooms; another to the operations departments, otherwise known as the "back office", where the accounting, legal, human resources and other services were located; and two floors for the managers, analysts and traders. No hierarchies, no committees, no eternal meetings. Almost 1,500 people to manage tens of billions of dollars, and one boss: the owner.

The founder of this investment fund was one of the few people I would dare call a genius. Like other renowned managers of large hedge funds, he was known for his passion for mathematics and rigorous analysis, and his tendency to question established dogmas. He could absorb information like no one else, and he listened to everyone. His weapons were his obsession with work, and being alert 24 hours a day. And when something led him to make a mistake, he would get back on his feet, learn and become stronger. He began in the nineties while at university, with a little money loaned to him by his relatives. Instead of devoting himself to the big stock market party of those years, he went from bank to bank trying desperately to open short positions – that is, to borrow a high-price share in order to sell it and return it at a lower price if stock prices fall (also known as short selling).

At that time, at the height of the dot-com boom, with the stock market rising 2% every day, this sounded like madness. In 2005, his fund was managing more than $10 billion, and he ranked among the top three highest-earning managers, receiving $1.2 billion annually (according to the *Financial Times*).

Upon my arrival, I saw some young men leaving carrying boxes with personal stuff. Leaving. A good start.

"Give me six longs and six shorts" was the first request that Dylan made of me. He was a mathematician who, according to company legend, had a photographic memory.

A "long position" (or long selling) is a traditional investment: buying a security in the hope that it will go up or will perform better than the market. "Short selling" means to short a stock as I described before. It's sometimes inappropriately described 'as "bearish". This involves borrowing a security on interest, to then sell it, wait for it to fall or fair worse than the rest, buy it back again and return it to the broker. If the share has fallen, the difference is gained. But the chief aim of "shorts", in fact, is to cover the exogenous risk of the "long positions" – to mitigate the white noise effect that is caused by market volatility, also known as "beta".

He was asking me to run a portfolio with an equal number of longs and shorts, which is what is known as a "neutral portfolio" – one that's not subject to any stock market movements but generates gains if your personal analysis is correct, regardless of which way the stock market goes. This type of portfolio yields profits, for example, if the six longs fall but fall less than the six shorts. This strategy is known as "market neutral", and it's my favourite, as it doesn't depend on Bernanke or Draghi or Merkel or Rajoy saying or doing anything in particular. We will discuss this at length in subsequent chapters.

The atmosphere in a hedge fund company is entirely unlike what we see in the movies. There are no men with glamorous hairstyles, wearing suits and braces, hollering into telephones. I was surprised by the silence and peacefulness of the environment. Most of the people were casually dressed. Most of the men were wearing polo shirts, chinos and white t-shirts. Everyone was doing their own thing: trying to make money. And there was I, like a jerk, dressed for a wedding.

All the analysts, managers and operators were communicating among themselves via Bloomberg instant messaging: an indispensable work tool for any manager or operator.[2] Besides the hundreds of screens providing real-time data on the prices of anything, this service has an application, similar to WhatsApp, through which subscribers can communicate live. It has the advantage that all conversations are recorded, meaning that no one can say they have misunderstood anything. This makes it extremely useful for the financial regulators, be they the SEC (Securities and Exchange Commission) or the FCA (Financial Conduct Authority). All background communications are carried out using this chat service.

The interviews took place throughout the day. I came across mathematicians, physicists, physicians, former government officials, retired members of the armed forces... I was asked questions of a professional and personal nature, over and over again, incessantly. No, I didn't get to eat.

The last interview was with the CIO, the chief investment officer. He asked me what I would do should I fail. I replied, "Acknowledge it and try not to fail again." He asked me two more questions: "What book are you currently reading?" and "What was the last film you saw?" After I answered, he got up and left. I was convinced that I had completely screwed up and responded hesitantly. I was unsure if I had been consistent with

---

[2] The Bloomberg Professional Service is, together with Reuters, the most comprehensive market data platform in the sector, and publishes prices of all manner of financial instruments in real time.

my earlier statements, when I had been asked the same question two or three times. In the afternoon, a car took me back to the airport.

When I got home, I told my wife about what had been the most surreal experience of my entire life. I must say that, on the one hand, the atmosphere was unnerving. On the other, however, the opportunity to surround oneself with so many brilliant minds posed a thrilling challenge.

On Monday, they called me again. "We'd like you to see some more people." Over the space of a month, I underwent a further six interview sessions, personality tests and all kinds of other tests. Clearly, they were looking for more than just a solid professional profile and a good knowledge of the market. They were searching for a specific way of understanding and analysing the world.

Then, suddenly, silence. I gave it up for lost.

One month later, while I was on a business trip to Copenhagen, the investment fund's head of human resources called me. "We'd love to make you an offer."

From what I was told, their decision to choose me from among the other candidates, despite being older and having fewer years' experience in the City, was what they called an ability to "think against the box". They were looking for someone who not only thought "*out* of the box", and so could come up with solutions that were different from what most people could dream up for the same problems, but also viewed problems *and* solutions in ways most never would.

I began to understand the reason for the diversity of profiles and why many of the successful managers did not come from traditional professional backgrounds. Alfred Winslow, credited as the original hedge fund manager, was a sociologist and journalist. Bill Gross – the king of bonds – studied psychology. André Kostolany read philosophy and art history. James Simons, of Renaissance Technologies, the world's most profitable hedge fund, was a mathematician. In many cases, the economist university degree and the typical master's degree don't help. Existing schools focus on orthodoxy, and a uniform, consensual, diplomatic, Keynesian vision of the economy. To be successful in an investment fund of this type requires a passion for the economy, but not orthodoxy or traditional analysis, and definitely not agreement with the majority opinion. It calls for seeing things from a unique point of view, and questioning established norms. This was how things such as the "subprime", the sovereign debt crisis, the dot-com and housing bubbles were discovered. It's also for this reason that those who come from outside the traditional economy but feel a passion for it are so successful. They are people who study and analyse everything in enormous detail from an objective, unique and independent point of view. It's about knowing how to question the standard estimate, counter traditional dogma and take risks.

I lived in the United States for a while before returning to London. When I arrived at the office on the first day, I found a six-screen computer terminal. One of them showed the portfolio they asked for at the first interview with six long positions and six short positions. It appears that on the day of my interview the hedge fund had invested a large amount on my recommendations, and throughout the entire selection process they had been generating either profits or losses. Luckily, the screen was green. Profit. I nearly had a heart attack.

I had joined a hedge fund. Let no one tell you that dreams don't come true. At thirty-six years of age.

CHAPTER TWO

THE FINANCIAL MARKET: COMPLEX AND VOLATILE

My decision to take the plunge into the financial world began around 2003. At that time, I often asked myself the following questions: "Why haven't we learnt anything from the Russian or Latin American economic crises we've just got through?"

After nearly ten years in an integrated oil company, where I worked in several departments from 1991 until 2000, I was put in charge of the investor relations department at a gas transmission company, where I took part in the company's initial public offering (IPO). I had some years of experience in corporate communications and investor relations management, but it was a fascinating experience to have direct involvement in the IPO of a company that at that time was unknown to the market. To work with investment banks, draw up the paperwork, understand what the main messages were that would have to be conveyed in order to make the company look attractive, analyse and revise the models and reports of the analysts, travel the world to explain the company's strategy... None of this was new to me, but to do it for a relatively unknown entity that had never even been listed gave me an entirely different perspective on things. Securing each little victory and achieving each target was complex and arduous.

The gas transmission company was very old school. It had never been listed or had quoted bonds and its team of managers not only lacked interest in the market but actually viewed it with suspicion. Fortunately, the company's chairman had first-hand knowledge and experience of the financial world. When he was in the oil sector, where we had previously met, he had participated in many IPOs and institutional trips (the so-called roadshows) to explain the company's strategy to prospective investors. He had prepared many presentations. I felt privileged to have the opportunity to work for a company that was to undertake a stock market launch for the first time, and to have the full support of an executive who perfectly understood this world, its needs and the crucial importance of financial disclosure. True, we had experience, but the task that lay ahead was monumental. We had to convince potential shareholders that a small, unknown company with sizeable risks and regulatory uncertainties was a good investment.

This was not easy. I recall, for example, a trip across the United States visiting far-flung places, such as Des Moines (Iowa) in the middle of the American heartland, to talk with a farmers' pension fund. At the end of the meeting, we flew immediately to another state where someone might want to listen to us. To place a small Spanish company on the stock market map is no easy feat. Many investors received our presentations with doubt, suspicion or outright boredom. We covered five states in four days and then returned to Europe to do six countries in another four days. We had to stand out from the thousands of securities that were competing for capital. And the only way to do this was by being better, more transparent and more committed.

It was like having a huge white canvas and a palette of colours to create the picture we had always wanted to paint. Over those years, we set up an investor relations office, we organised shareholder meetings, did all the paperwork and everything else we could to put the company on the map. Thanks to an outstanding team, which is still there today, the share price doubled in three years, and today it continues to be one of the few Spanish IPOs since 2001 that has created value for the shareholder, despite the enormous uncertainties surrounding the group's results, the lack of regulation and the fact that some of the major shareholders have had to reduce their ownership positions.

The successes we achieved in that time – including several awards for the Best Work in Investor Relations and the Best Offer of Securities to the Public of the year – cemented my interest in and passion for the financial markets. And so we arrive at the year 2003.

Spain was experiencing a boom. Everything was going up, and Europe looked on enviously and held us up as an example of an economic miracle. Our companies got bigger by the day, absorbing all kinds of foreign companies at high prices. Debt had increased by 200% since 1996 and the world was our oyster. Despite having been through the Latin American crisis a few years earlier, which left many conglomerates on the verge of bankruptcy, we went on to conquer the world... accumulating debt. Suddenly, your next-door neighbour was an expert in property, shares and investments. "In the long term, everything goes up."

Maybe I was an oddball, but I noted something was amiss. None of this tallied. And numbers that did not tally were very important to me, and would be even more so in the future. We had overlooked the balance sheet and forgotten the importance of debt. I still recall a conversation with a senior executive of a listed company who explained to me, without blushing, that the debt from the recent strategic acquisitions undertaken by the company "should not be taken into account", because "when we sell at much higher prices we repay it and even generate a profit". We were dominated by the so-called greater fool theory, which states that after a malinvestment or an expensive purchase someone, preferably foreign, will always turn up who will purchase at an even higher price.

In conversations with my friends, I was always told, "You're wrong, Daniel. This can and will continue." Few people doubted that it was possible to experience annual growth levels of three per cent for the next 20 years. I was very dubious.

An enlightening crisis and a real shock

I should say the reason I doubted that Spain's boom would be long-lived was because I had witnessed the Argentine crisis of 1999 to 2001, after which my children were born. Yes, triplets after a crisis that almost swept away the company for which I had spent a decade working. For some reason, my sense of caution and perception of the risk were dramatically affected. That shock led us from being praised for strategic transactions of international envy to searching for ways of securing liquidity on a daily basis. These experiences are never forgotten.

Before the crisis – which produced the massive devaluation of the Argentine peso – we were on cloud nine. After it, the successes, the bonanza, the euphoria, the feeling that "everything is going well" vanished and we had to deal with the basic problem of survival. This situation had such an impact on the company that a number of investment banks began to cast doubt on the group's future. Experiencing the Latin American crisis and learning from the corporate managers who saved the company from disaster helped me focus on what is really important when analysing a security, bond or country.

We love vague expressions such as "The company is a global leader", "It's always been like this" and "Everything will turn out all right in the end", and we forget the figures. What really counts is the cash, the balance sheet, the debt, the working capital.

Liquidity and solvency. However, just three years after the Latin American shock, few seemed to remember those indicators. Business schools frequently discuss concepts like "increasing debt to lower the cost of capital" or "creating value by leveraging an asset". These ideas are correct to a degree, but cease to be so if one forgets the debt saturation threshold, that is the moment when an additional unit of indebtedness does not generate positive marginal returns but negative ones.

And we forget. In 2014, barely six years after the biggest financial crisis since 1929, we are back to complacency and are forgetting debt and solvency ratios.

In England, they say: "Hope for the best, but prepare for the worst." I had the impression that Spain had bypassed all security checks, and that all the lessons learnt from previous economic crises had been forgotten. All the Spanish autonomous communities acquired the right to more debt, an airport, a high-speed rail link. They all had to have the same economic model for growth, the same limitless resources. The same happened in Greece, Portugal, Italy and Ireland. Debt created the illusion of wealth. The US Federal Reserve announced the tapering, or partial withdrawal, of monetary stimulus in 2015, after almost two trillion dollars had been spent. However, despite a low 6.3% unemployment rate, the US showed the lowest labour participation rate since 1978 and 11 million people *taken out* of the labour market and not counted as *unemployed.*

What is the problem? Monetary policy has not benefited the ordinary citizen, only financial market participants. But the risks are paid by the citizens. Easy money has inflated financial assets, and the cost of reducing unnecessary expansionary policies was met by heaping massive financial burdens on ordinary taxpayers.

The middle class lost in the crisis, but had almost no access to the easy money of the quantitative easing (QE) years and will likely pay the hangover when this new credit bubble bursts.

In those years between 2005 and 2008 few spoke of the housing bubble, and fewer still of the infrastructure bubble that went hand in hand with those ever-growing demand estimates: an excess in infrastructures that I discussed in my articles in the press. No one asked where the money would come from, let alone how it would be returned.

The sensible managers, those who warned of this wasteful spending spree, were removed from their posts for being party poopers. I was fortunate to learn and grow professionally alongside some of these prudent managers, with experience of how to deal with cycles and crises. So, like them, that optimism paid for with debt made me shudder.

The fact is that in 2008 we returned to the same pre-Argentina euphoria and I began to get the jitters. I had been making plans for a big change that I had spent years mulling over since I began to work in the investor relations office. I spent eight years doing this in the two companies I mentioned. My duties consisted of coordinating the company's communications and reporting and attending to the share and bond investors on a daily basis. This experience opened my eyes to the reality of the financial sector and the different operators working in it, from the investment banks to the ratings agencies, debt and equity investors, the competing companies and the different sectors. Above all, it gave me the opportunity to better grasp something that most people do not perceive: the true nature of the markets. How they think, what they seek, what their concerns are.

One of the first lessons of my experience was to understand the nature of the economic information that we receive. Most of the information that reaches market participants is reactive: it only explains what has happened. What's more, such information is belated, filtered, often massaged and sometimes tainted by politics and social relations.

It's no coincidence it's called "the market".

The big question I'm often asked is "Who or what really are 'the financial markets'?" The best definition I have ever found was given to me by my good friend Marc Garrigasait, a fund manager at Koala Capital. It is this: "Your mother's savings." More precisely, the financial markets are the savings of the entire world's fathers and mothers, although the savings with the most sway belong to the fathers and mothers from countries that have the most assets and can loan them to, or invest them in, other countries. The pension funds, which are charged with ensuring that a lifetime's savings are not lost, invest the money they hold via the "financial markets" in bonds, stocks, commodities and currencies as core assets. The managers of these huge pension funds must ensure they get a reasonable annual return so that when families retire they receive the highest amount possible. So if they fear that the money loaned to (bonds), or invested (shares or stocks) in, a country or specific company may be lost, they immediately withdraw it and invest in or loan to another country or business that conveys more confidence and greater seriousness. Another part of the market are countries that hold vast sums of money as a result of their surpluses, such as China, India, Brazil, Russia or Norway, which invest astronomic sums in bonds and shares from the leading Western countries.

My son Daniel, upon learning that his grandmother was about to publish her first book, coined the slogan "Make my grandma happy: buy her novel." This simple expression allowed me to fathom the soul of the market. It's a selling process and there are two parts to this business: the supplier and the customer. The seller appeals to our emotional instinct to win clients. Make my grandmother happy. Buy government bonds for the good of the country. Buy shares in company X for their contribution to society.

Companies, governments, investment banks and analysts are all sellers in this market. They sell their product to the buyers, that is investors and ordinary people, who are themselves consumers of the "goods" that these entities sell. It's very important to understand this, because failure to understand the selling nature of some agents can lead us to misinterpret or overestimate the information we receive.

In a shopping centre with many different displays, intermediaries and end customers, the seller always strives to showcase the best qualities of their product. The seller is optimistic and tends to offer us a positive outlook. Similarly, and though today we don't perceive it as such, the market functions according to positive impulses. It's something that stems from human nature itself, which needs both to believe in the long term in order to survive and to feel optimistic and receive encouraging news, even in the face of adverse events.

Therefore, the market, rather than trying to deceive, appeals to human nature's yearning for growth and betterment. So sellers put on their best face for their product, as people do for family snapshots where they always look happy, or in advertising, which always displays an attractive image. They are like the father who thinks his child is the brightest and the one who will go furthest in the world.

Between the sellers and buyers, there are a number of agents or intermediaries who facilitate financial trading operations. First, there are the brokers, agents who are charged with finding a counterparty for their clients. These agents are mere intermediaries who just match buy and sell orders and take a commission on both transactions. Brokers may be small firms or big banks. Then there are the dealers, or negotiators, who have a more active role in the process. These agents trade with their clients, that is they buy and sell securities. What they've bought from or sold to one client they can then sell to or buy from another. Brokers offer their clients liquidity, and run the risk that prices move against them before they are able to pass on their products.

Many of these intermediaries are concentrated in investment banks – the main ones being Goldman Sachs, JPMorgan, Bank of America, Merrill Lynch and Citigroup, yet they also operate in traditional banks like Santander, Barclays and HSBC. These banks also offer fixed income and equity analysis, economic studies and corporate assistance services to companies who want access to the markets in order to be able to issue shares and debt.

Inside this machinery, the banks act like oil for the engine. They are essential to ensure the financial system's smooth running. We forget about them when everything is going well, because we take for granted the liquidity and the instant access to financial transactions we enjoy. When a client decides to sell or buy, they never doubt they will find a counterparty. It is taken for granted.

Banks actually do a very difficult job. They put together the savings and deposits of participants with short- to medium-term liquidity needs and return expectations with the demand for credit from participants with longer-term requirements.

We forget the basic importance of the banks as intermediaries because we assume that liquidity is guaranteed and that it will always exist. We only remember the banks for the problems they cause, which of course must be recognised and solved. And we forget that the banking system is the most regulated of sectors.

Yes, the European financial crisis is not a crisis of deregulation or private banks; 50% of European financial institutions were semi state-owned or controlled by politicians in 2006. There have been thousands of pages of regulations published every year since the creation of the European Union and the European Banking Authority (EBA). Regulation and supervision in Europe is enormous. Since 1999 and based on documents produced by the EBA, EU and European Central Bank (ECB), that's 180 new rules a week.

And as I will come on to argue, the crisis was born of an economic model too dependent on commercial banks with total assets that exceeded 320% of the eurozone's combined gross domestic product (GDP) within a deeply integrated system. Excessive, complex and bureaucratic regulation has prolonged the agony of the industry for many years, instead of facilitating market conditions for the capital increases and asset sales needed.

Despite the detailed and complex regulation of the eurozone, between 2008 and 2011 Europe spent €4.5 trillion (37% of the GDP of the EU) in aid to financial institutions, many of them public and highly regulated.

More regulation will not solve the problem.

Europe's banks suffer what is called an "endogeneity problem" (read the excellent analysis *Regulation of European Banks and Business Models* published by the Centre for European Policy Studies). It is precisely this excessive intervention which prevents a quick and surgical solution to the financial sector's difficulties. Regulation must be effective and simple. In Europe, it is not.

Banks play an essential role in a market driven by the perception of growth and prosperity.

The market simply reflects that human nature of which we spoke earlier, regardless of whether we see things from the point of view of the sellers or intermediaries. So I find it hilarious when people speak of "attacks" by the market. More than 67% of the funds under management are exclusively "long-only", so they only enter the market as buyers. And in hedge funds, which we will analyse later, the average net long exposure (bullish) rarely goes below 30% of total funds.

Just as governments, companies and investment banks play the role of sellers and intermediaries, so do investors play the role of customers. And as such, they can make a mistake when choosing a product. So they also take on certain levels of risk.

And as clients, they have every right to expect a lot from what they buy. When we forget that the market is a triangular seller–product–client relationship, and assume that we are within our rights to expect to find a seller for poor-quality products, the chain of value and confidence begins to break.

Understanding that the seller–client relationship in the financial markets is identical to that of any other business activity has been invaluable for me to carrying out the transition from the business world to banking and investment management. Be your product a sovereign bond or a company share, it's absolutely imperative to understand and evaluate the needs of your clients and to strive to offer competitive, quality goods and then attract clients and capital, and not wait for it to rain down from heaven.

What was it that fascinated me about those investors who came to see our company? In the meetings with the senior management, they were not afraid to pose awkward questions and to turn balance sheets, ideas, forecasts, past performances and the like on their heads. At first I wondered: "How dare they speak so frankly and so directly to our chairman, CEO, CFO, who within the company and the country are treated almost like royalty?" But these were our clients, current or prospective. They had every right to do so, and were only expressing their concerns. They wanted to analyse and understand what could happen, not what had already happened.

An investor is your client. He is not doing you a favour or making a donation. He is taking a risk: investing his money and seeking to maximise the possibilities of obtaining a profit with respect to the risk he takes. And our product is one of thousands from which he can choose on the world market. Not only must we outshine the others in image and in current figures; we must lend credibility to our "proud father" expectations that our product will grow into something strong and healthy.

I remember a meeting with a leading international investor. His biggest worry was not "How much will I make?" but "How much do I stand to lose?"

It was during this learning curve that I realised that in continental Europe the concept of open and transparent communication was still rather rudimentary. This was perhaps due to the existence of majority shareholders and the generalised absence of mutual interests between actors on the buy-side (above all, companies) and clients (minority shareholders). The protectionist environment had not changed.

This experience led me to seek an opportunity to change my career and attempt to go over to the investor side: to become a client, a risk-taker. I also considered my career and my professional profile. I had spent the last 12 years at two companies and felt the need to branch out, add experiences and gain knowledge that could lead me to positions where I might improve my independence and, naturally, earn more money.

The opportunity to put this decision into action came from the market.

After three months of fruitless searches, I was contacted by a head-hunter to discuss the possibility of leaving Spain in order to work as an analyst in a London investment bank, in the City.

It was an opportunity worth considering. To gain a foothold in the financial markets, in particular in the City, is incredibly difficult. If you're given the possibility to get into that environment, you should think seriously about the answer you will give. To let that train pass by could have closed up a direct avenue to securing my long-term goal.

During the interview with the head-hunter, he asked me where I saw myself five years from now, and I replied, "Working in a hedge fund." The head-hunter looked at me in amazement. He told me it was a very ambitious and terribly difficult goal. Not only that, he warned me that more than half the hedge fund managers are fired every two years. "Be careful what you wish for", he said.

The decision was not easy. From my secure position as a director at a good company, with little risk and a stable environment, I was to become an analyst, which meant taking a step down the hierarchical ladder and moving into an extremely competitive sector, fraught with risk and with much of my salary dependent on bonuses for meeting targets.

I would be taking one step back in order to take three steps forward in the medium term. It was a risky decision, but one that would allow me to be what I wanted to be: an investor (and, of course, enjoy the remuneration that came with it). My decision process was undeniably influenced by this overarching personal ambition.

If you want to get into the financial world, you have to like money and you have to want to earn lots of it. If your aims are to "broaden my experience", "meet people" and "study other sectors in detail", there are thousands of jobs out there. You must know why you are there and what other people are there for. All of them. I was not going to work for an NGO or for an engineering firm. I was about to enter the "money-making market".

I recall the conversation with my family when I announced that, at my age (late thirties), with three newborn babies (triplets), I was renouncing a cushy, secure, well-paid executive position in the corporate world, the dream of any son's mother, in order to try my luck in London. Of course, everyone I knew told me it was a mistake, that it was risky, that I should not give up a certain quantity for the great unknown... the usual clichés.

In the book *The New Market Wizards: Conversations with America's Top Traders*, by Jack D. Schwager, all the participants agree that to be successful one needs to have a magnificent relationship with, and the support of, one's partner. My own experience supported this finding. My wife and I had to have a common goal and a clear objective and to be willing to take risks, even be separated for a time, if I was to be ultimately successful with my career change.

At that time everyone told us it was crazy, but I had made up my mind.

I flew to London, leaving my family in Spain. At the weekends, whenever I could, I would get up at four in the morning and fly back to see them for a few hours, then return to London on the Sunday at midnight. After two years of weekly commuting, my wife gave up her job as a manager at an investment firm to look after the children and come to London, where it's almost impossible to combine work and family life on account of the timetables, holidays and demands of the British private school system. We went from having two sizeable steady incomes to the uncertainty of the City and the gamble of annual bonuses and variable remuneration.

You may have read the sad story of a bank intern in the City of London who died in 2013 after allegedly working 72 hours straight. If you read about it in the papers, you will probably have been horrified by the description of "inhuman hours", deaths and suicide in the financial sector. Nothing could be further from the truth.

Life in the City is tough, and employers demand results, as it should be. Imagine for a second that the person who manages your savings or your pension fund was remunerated by any other measure than profitability. Would you invest in this fund? Work can be strenuous, but slavery-type hours and inhuman conditions are a fiction. Yes, the day begins very early, at six or seven o'clock. But anyone who takes the train at Waterloo Station or the tube at Bank or Liverpool Street knows that at five or six p.m. the vast majority of people are on their way home.

Everyone in the City has had to work long hours and several weekends, but so do entrepreneurs, writers, musicians and journalists.

I'm afraid that behind the controversy over the City's death lies more demagoguery than real concern for working too hard. In the same way that no one questions an elite athlete who trains aggressively or a singer who performs at 250 concerts in a row, few question the long hours required of skilled professionals giving of their best in a highly competitive industry.

Professionals who go through a very thorough selection process freely take the responsibility, because it is also a passion. This is not just work. It is a meritocracy and competition is encouraged. The same thing that many call sacrifice is, for the vast majority in the City, a pleasure.

Working in the City is a conscious and free decision. Whoever does not like the system should not worry, because they would probably never be hired. However, between a free and competitive work environment and a safe but frustrating one, there is something about which I am very clear: I would not trade freedom for security. Never.

Today, we are told that we were very lucky and that it was a good move. It was neither luck nor madness. It was about taking risks and being prepared to make sacrifices. More than ten years later, I can say that I have a full life, a wonderful family and my work is not a burden, because I love it. The day it becomes a burden I will quit, and I'm sure there will be dozens of candidates happy to take my place. Freely.

CHAPTER THREE

WELCOME TO LONDON

I left my family in Madrid and rented a tiny apartment next to the London Stock Exchange that had no central heating, and where on at least one occasion I was visited by some mice from the kitchen of the coffee shop below. Far from glamorous. But I had to save, as I had three newborns. The aim of this adventure was not to live the life of a character out of Oliver Stone's *Wall Street*. It was about work, work and then some more work.

I was hired as a financial analyst. I had barely any experience in the field. Of course, I had read thousands of reports and knew many analysts, but I lacked expertise, including knowledge of how to do financial modelling.

The Liverpool Street building was imposing. Huge, all glass, people streaming in and out of its doors day and night. The trading room commanded respect. Hundreds of sales executives and traders closing deals. I had seen it many times, but had never realised the power and energy it gave off. I had arrived.

I imagined there would be some kind of training, some period of adaptation, some help. Well, no. They showed me where I would work, in a row together with dozens of analysts who were talking on the phone, entering data on Excel spreadsheets and drafting reports. I was given a telephone and everything I needed, and set to work.

It was a complete culture shock. No training courses, no meetings to see how you were faring, no progress evaluation. I was with everyone and against everyone. The financial world is fiercely competitive, totally Darwinian. It's not a trade union environment; collectivist, familiar and comfortable. No one wants to waste time. It's assumed that you have been taken on for your skill, that you are able to generate the expected results and that you are sufficiently capable and self-reliant to achieve this without constant mentoring. If your work is not the best quality, someone else who has achieved better results will pick up your annual bonus.

So I took it as a personal battle. I would not fail.

I thought back to my first day at university. A teacher came into the classroom and said: "Be aware that I will fail an average of 80% of the class." At that moment, I knew it was me against him. I took the same approach at the beginning of my time in London. I viewed it as a personal battle and completely immersed myself in achieving my objectives, of being one of those who succeeded. Quite frankly, I had an awful time of it, and there were many occasions when I regretted being there, in that dreadful apartment with my family thousands of kilometres away, when I could have been calmly working in my permanent, comfortable, secure position in Spain.

My first major challenge was to pass the FCA (Financial Conduct Authority) exam, in order to be able to operate in the markets. It makes me furious when I read in the press that the financial markets are not well regulated and that investors and analysts are given free rein like cowboys. I would make those people all study for the exams of the CFA or the CIIA (international qualifications of financial analysts), and of course I would have them all study for – and pass – the FCA exams. Day after day, hour after hour, studying the details of one of the world's most complex and detailed set of regulations. At my age. Thirty-five. A fully fledged former Spanish company director wearing a Hermès tie and a blue suit. How ironic.

"I will not fail. I'm not going back to Spain. I'm not the dumbest of all those who are here, so my options are to pass or pass, there's no alternative." And I passed. The first assault.

My strategy was crystal clear. Maximise the advantage of having worked on "the other side", in the corporate world; of having spent years dealing with investors; of my knowledge of the internal processes of companies: how they think, what they fear, what their investment strategies are. And at the same time, use this experience to learn everything and more on financial modelling, multiples and ratios, and absorb all I could from what my colleagues were doing. I would be analysing companies and their numbers, but my experience would come in useful in identifying how they presented them and why.

Valuation models

When you read in the newspaper that a company has sold an asset or bought something, it's hard to know for certain if this news will have a real impact on the share price. It's easy to make a mistake by attributing undue importance to the news or, worse still, giving credibility to our initial reaction. To have a good understanding of market developments, we need models. They need not be overly complex, yet if you create your own models I'm sure you will avoid investment errors and overrating the news on many occasions.

The most important thing for analysts is to create a model that allows them to analyse the company's results. In order to gain a correct understanding of what it is that is having a real impact on the company's results and profitability, it is essential to develop simulations with which we may feel comfortable, be they individual, sectorial or macroeconomic. A model is not a clock that always gives exact responses, but an evaluation tool that, naturally, includes data and forecasts that are personal to the analyst who creates it. It should draw on two types of data:

- current and past economic information provided by the company or country;
- short-, medium- and long-term forecasts, either personal forecasts or those provided by external agencies and consultants.

There are many types of models, yet the principal framework basically consists of five segments:

- Macroeconomic forecasts and external inputs. These are estimates of the environment external to the company itself, from the GDP of the countries in which the company operates to commodity prices, currency exchange rates, inflation and so on.
- Current and past data on revenues, cash flow and balance sheets. All this data is gathered from public reports, annual accounts, companies and states.
- Medium-term forecasts supplied by the country or the company. They are taken from strategic plans and public budgets.
- Medium-term forecasts based on our own perception of the aforementioned forecasts. It is crucial to try to gauge, with our own tools, whether the company or country will remain above or below its own forecast. We should remember that both companies and countries are reactive when giving information. For example, in 2008, in the midst of the crisis, most companies stated that their businesses had not been affected and that their plans would be maintained. Four years later,

more than half of them have lowered both their forecasts and dividends.

• Comprehensive evaluation: the sum of the parts or valuations of assets, solvency ratios, liquidity. This comprehensive analysis tells us whether a country or a company is profitable, solvent and attractive.

I won't dwell on model building, as this is not the subject of this book, but for more information I recommend *Financial Modeling and Valuation: A Practical Guide to Investment Banking and Private Equity* by Paul Pignataro (Wiley Finance) and *Financial Modeling* by Simon Benninga (MIT Press).

So there I was, fighting to gain a foothold, and learning on the job how to draw up forecasts and to interact with my clients: the sellers and the corporate bankers. The best advice I received was from three friends: Harold, one of the best analysts in the City and battle-hardened after many years in finance; Lem, a broker who began in the eighties and was known as "Mr Floatation", as he was capable of placing any stock of any company among his clients; and John, a salesman in an investment bank who was a remarkable expert at summarising any analysis, regardless of its complexity, in a few lines in a way that attracted clients. The three worked together for a German bank before each went his own way, and at that time as a team they were called "The Three Too: Too Fat, Too Tall and Too White". No, the financial market does not adhere to political correctness.

Lem, for example, was sometimes so good at pushing an IPO that he even allowed himself to joke about it. He would sell shares in Hell if it floated. Harold and Lem's knowledge of the inner workings of the City was second to none. They had seen the good times, the private jets, the restaurant bills amounting to thousands of pounds and the bonuses with which they were able to buy a house in a month without a mortgage. Yet they'd been through the bad times as well, when 50,000 people were laid off every quarter, when people turned up for work only to find their office entry card no longer functioned and were told they could pick up the box containing their personal belongings and go home, when professionals with years of experience lost their lifetime's savings because their banks' shares had plummeted.

Lem had a unique personality. He was a burly Scotsman who, despite his wry sense of humour, was loyal, supportive and friendly. He arrived in the City by chance, when he was giving electric guitar lessons to a banker who noticed his potential and talent. Lem went on to hold such sway that he allowed himself to tell the CEO of an important bank that she would be more successful in her meetings with investors if she wore a miniskirt, and to tell a CEO that if he posted a photo of himself eating a Big Mac he would create a more approachable image.

Harold was a master analyst. He was unrivalled in his knowledge of different companies and his sector, and oozed financial analysis from every pore. Like so many, he also came to the market by chance. He had been hired by a company whose strategy division he ran to cover a range of different sectors, and after years of fighting, he was for me a benchmark of professional rigour, camaraderie and generosity, despite also being a competitor!

"Consensus will only lead you to mediocrity," the three of them told me. Think outside the box and question dogma, because to maintain the consensus estimates, to stay in the sheepfold, will only lead you to mediocrity.

Indeed, Harold had lived through the golden age of the City, when the money flowed like water. Although he had also witnessed the years in which the operators waited one by one, like lambs to the slaughter, to see the director of the bank to learn whether they were included on the list of staff to be fired, whether they would receive an indemnity package, whether they had time to find another job. "It's war, and each quarter the bodies pile up. The time of easy money ended a long, long time ago, and the only thing that will save you is to stand out from the rest." And this is how I approached it: to come in like a bull in a china shop and try to do away with the dogmas that prevailed among the community of analysts, who were above all competitors, despite also being friends.

What is the "consensus"? As I have said, the human being needs to be positive and maintain hopeful forecasts. And the market reflects this need. Consensus is the weighted average of the analysts' estimates and recommendations on any one item, commodities price, bonds or macroeconomics forecasts. Consensus means tranquillity: "The economic results of company X or country Y are in line with the analysts' estimates" (even though all these analysts may have had to gradually "cut/ lower" their estimates for company X or country Y until they achieved an acceptable consensus). In consensus, everyone is happy. The equidistance and the group's reassurance is part of the financial game.

A relevant percentage of analysts do the same. They reproduce, almost literally, the information that the companies, the governments and the agencies supply them with, and publish with great preference positive and bullish opinions: buy, buy, buy. It's the sell-side. It matters little if they are wrong. If you take the forecasts and recommendations of any investment bank in any country, you will discover a rough average of 65% buy recommendations, and at most 15% recommendations to sell. And then there is the most curious recommendation of all: "hold" – equal weight – neither hot nor cold, neither white nor black. Tepid.

Living by consensus estimate was not my style. I wanted be a leading analyst, like the genius who discovered that Enron had gone bankrupt while others were saying it was the best of the best. Harold had concluded that the estimates of two companies he was following were inflated by 25%. When I worked in the oil sector, Sue, Irene, Caroline or Jeremy drafted extremely uncompromising yet fair analyses in spite of the letters of complaint that the directors of these entities sent to the banks where they worked. Friends – like Alastair, James, Fred, Louise, Bosco, Raimundo and Jesús – would not give in to intimidation by companies and governments and wrote what they believed regardless and with rigour, and they had dared to write negative reports on firms with whom their bank had important business.

Moreover, I looked to those who, like my friend Alejandro, had unearthed hidden gems; undiscovered securities for the general public that would rise between 100 and 120%. These were my pacesetters. The big ones. The independents. Those who made financial analysis thrilling, not those who wrote insipid and drab articles for consumption.

Curiously, in analysis it's sometimes not that important if you make a mistake with a positive recommendation because, as in advertising, the buyers look beyond the recommendation, scrutinise the data and read between the lines. As with any product, they read the information and draw their own conclusions. Is the information credible? How does it differ from that of the rest of the analysts?

Accurate downbeat forecasts, on the other hand, sell little and generate unpleasant consequences. If an analyst says that everything is going downhill, the vast majority of clients simply will not listen, even if the forecast is correct. Don't blame the banks and the analysts. The clients are also to blame, because they demand a very specific type of product. And this product, in most cases, is like the adverts on British television, where the sun always shines even though outside it never stops raining.

I recall a conversation with the research director of a large national corporation. Asking him how he saw things, he replied:

"I'm preparing a study on the economic situation, but it needs some positive spin. The board doesn't want to hear anything gloomy, it makes them very cranky." The same trend pervades the whole chain of the market. And that's why the crises are so acute and supposedly unpredictable. States, companies and investors are always "excellently prepared for growth"; everyone is a good manager in times of plenty. However, there are few good crisis managers or market operators, on the side of buyers or sellers, willing to listen to bad news and understand economic cycles.

This trend, fortunately, has changed over the years, and it has contributed to improving the quality and independence of the analysis one can find in blogs, social networks and webpages like CNBC's Squawk Box, Zero Hedge, Seeking Alpha or Business Insider. The analysis has more critical weight, the banking is more independent and the recommendations, despite remaining mostly upbeat, are more varied.

I soon found the formula for positioning myself in the market: to reveal in detail everything I thought was not known, especially when my experience in the energy sector could provide added value.

My first analysis report had to be a hit. Day after day, night after night, over many weekends, I worked non-stop until I completed 110 pages in which I set out in detail the functioning of the southern European energy sector. The opening sentence of the report read: "The war among pressure groups to change the electricity sector continues", and it went on to warn of the government's drive to halt liberalisation and encourage the construction of surplus capacity. Above all, I endeavoured to provide all the figures possible, as well as detailing any potential impact on companies' results in the event of changes in regulation, demand or price.

My reports were pretty successful, and despite being a newcomer to the City and working in a medium-sized bank, the clients were constantly calling me to ask for my opinion. That I always avoided political correctness and published what I thought, even when they disagreed, was highly valued. It's important to understand that clients (namely investors) value comprehensive, personal and independent analysis. This is what I quickly learnt, and I had the good fortune to establish good relations with the largest pension and hedge fund managers in the world, including the one that hired me a year and a half later. Some of these relationships are now friendships, but at that time I was looking to learn. Learn every day. Accept criticism, negative and positive feedback and strive to improve. Above all, I wanted to learn, not to impose my ideas. It was a stage and process that I soaked up like a sponge.

Now that I am on the client side and write in the press with total freedom, when going through my old reports I find it hard to believe what niceties we analysts had to use to be able to make our opinion known. I recall the filters that we had to go through before publishing: there were entire departments given over to compliance (editing and revising) to ensure that everything we wrote was in accordance with the legal rules of conduct and transparency of both the bank and the regulator.

We should never forget that by definition economic analysis is subjective. There is no wholly objective analysis. The crucial thing is that it should make sense and be well argued, to form the basis for debate, whether with clients or among economists. People who expect objectivity start from a misconception. The study of economic reality and above all forecasts always go through a subjective filter, in which experience, opinion and intellectual process all have a bearing. The important thing is that whoever reads it recognises that the process is logical and coherent, and that the opinion is both rational and ethical.

It's a shame, but we are used to living in highly planned economies and to thinking that economic cycles are unjustified anomalies, speculative movements or manipulations. We are afraid of economic cycles because we demand certainty and security, yet we don't grasp that planning and interventionism do not work in a globalised world. When an intervention takes place in one area, it subverts the natural process of economic development in another. Economic cycles are essential and must be thoroughly understood, because today all economies are intimately linked. Also, it is an error of judgement to take what we are told at face value, to believe that the chief economic agents have everything under control and can influence the future. Think of the sentence "Don't fight the Fed" so often read in blogs and articles. Central-bank-led market moves are important, undoubtedly, but fundamentals do matter and complacency can create very bad investment decisions based on "it can only go up because of a central bank's intervention".

The average person has trouble understanding that variables are dynamic, and that policies aimed at holding back or altering a variable often gives rise to exponential effects on the rest of the indicators. When interest rates, or money supply, are artificially manipulated, or new taxes are introduced, the impact is felt along the entire length of the economic chain, including business decisions, for better or for worse.

When we understand that the major economic players (governments, central banks, companies) have three principal characteristics, it becomes easier to understand the reality of economic cycles. They are sellers (seeking to sell a product), reactive (they manage things once events have occurred) and, above all, they hold an optimistic view of the future, hence the overriding importance of thinking "against the box". It's about identifying inconsistencies and cyclical changes, or at least understanding the level of risk to which we are exposing ourselves and studying the possible solutions to problems.

Today, in my daily work as a portfolio manager, when I am given a report I am not interested in the recommendation to "buy" or "sell". I am interested in the last three or four pages, the figures. I am interested in the analysis, why it draws the conclusion it does and on what basis it does so. I read more and more reports that differ from the consensus, with provocative and well-thought-through views from analysts, and I am glad to perceive that there is an ongoing improvement in the quality and independence of analysis.

My style of questioning everything and not letting myself be shaped by dogmas does not make my life particularly easy. Many people get annoyed and many internal and external forces try to make one fall in line with the majority. I can't say things have been bad, quite the reverse, but it's been no bed of roses. I had some interesting episodes, not least for my analysis of a famous takeover bid, entitled "Better Standalone Value", in which I wrote of the destruction of value brought about by the mergers in the energy sector, and in which I concluded that the value of the individual firms would be higher than that of the future entity, and certainly much higher than that of consensus estimates. This analysis was absolutely neutral, and provided accurate recommendations, yet created some controversy.

However, my analysis also generated several calls from investment funds that fast-tracked my plan to move into the fund management world in three or four years to become reality in the span of just a year and a half.

I am convinced that one of the reasons why there is broad consensus, that comfortable anonymity in which one seeks shelter with the others, is to avoid the potential risks entailed in challenging the status quo. And this is also why the top analysts, those who think differently, will always be heard if their arguments are coherent. I, of course, did not come anywhere near that elite, as I quickly moved to the buy-side. Mind you, what I learnt in that year-and-a-half stint in London as an investment bank analyst would me serve me well throughout my life.

CHAPTER FOUR

THE MARKET DOESN'T ATTACK, IT DEFENDS ITSELF

With artificial interest rates, we get an artificial economy driven by malinvestment leading to inevitable bubbles.

Ron Paul

I began writing for *El Confidencial* and collaborating with CNBC after my time at the US hedge fund (my articles are translated into English on my website, dlacalle.com). In 2007, I was hired by another London investment fund and in my spare time I shared my thoughts on macroeconomic issues and markets in my blog. My relationship, now a friendship, with the owners of *El Confidencial* arose from a series of emails in which I gave them my views on stock market and macroeconomic issues. One day while I was on a trip to Spain, we met for a coffee at the Hotel Palace in Madrid. They made me an offer to write a weekly column on the energy sector. It seemed like a great idea. Thus, my blog was born.

Between 2008 and 2009, I wrote exclusively on oil, electricity and energy policy. However, when the European sovereign debt crisis exploded, one day I felt tired of reading titles like "the markets are attacking Europe" and "speculators sink the stock markets" and started to write about general themes. In my first contribution, entitled "Week of panic, decade of binge, year of hangover",[3] I described how the market crashes and the bursting of the sovereign bubble stemmed from the unjustified wastage of the past. Since then, my goal has been to shed some light on how the market sees things, and why instead of demonising the markets we should learn to understand commercial and financial relations and know that the investors are our clients.

Hence my battle cry – "The market doesn't attack, it defends itself" – was born.

We love the market as long as everything is going well, there's lots of money sloshing about, the economy is growing and prices are rising. The senior managers slap one another on the back for their sound management "endorsed by the markets" and governments congratulate themselves for their "excellent credit rating" and the huge inflow of foreign capital. Everyone takes credit for the success.

Governments and politicians, furthermore, are absolutely convinced that the market can be manipulated and that the economy and its cycles can be modified by their management, yet they never take accountability for the consequences. As Ronald Reagan said, the most dangerous words are: "Hi, I'm from the government and I'm here to help."[4]

We are extreme capitalists, especially when the markets are on the rise. But when things are not looking good, the markets that were once "a true reflection of reality" become "evil" and we demand to be rescued from the losses and debts that we incur. Capitalists on the rise; socialists on the fall.

---

[3] http://tinyurl.com/d5weqct

[4] "The ten most dangerous words in the English language are 'Hi, I'm from the government, and I'm here to help.'" Remarks to Representatives of the Future Farmers of America, 28 July 1988.

When I was a student in the eighties, everyone was a speculator. Families, businesses, trades unions, political parties, banks. There was the property speculator ("Property prices never fall"), the stock market speculator ("Everything rises in the long term"), the state speculator ("Government bonds not only give good returns, they never fail"), the business speculator ("Don't worry about buying dear – what matters is to sell even dearer") and the imperialist speculator ("Our companies are taking over the world"). The European Union in the 90s was the market on steroids. For example, Spain was "the country where it was easiest to make your fortune", in the words of one minister of economy.

When the stock market rose, it was due to "investors"; when it fell, it was due to "the speculators". If a company takes out a loan twenty times the value of its capital in order to buy part of another, it "invests", but if you buy a share and then sell it, you "speculate". Surprising.

The media only remembers the markets and banks when things go wrong. Why? Because we are in an economy in which financial trading is despised for ideological reasons. The media speaks of the "real economy", as if the financial economy was not an essential element of the growth of world commerce and of the globalisation that we all enjoy and criticise in equal measure. We still don't value liquidity, access to capital and interconnectedness. They are taken for granted. They exist as if by magic.

The market does not attack, it defends itself, because it seeks to protect its currency and preserve its capital, in the face of a global policy of "financial repression".

Financial repression. This economic term, which the economists Carmen Reinhart and Kenneth Rogoff use constantly, refers to the policies of tax hikes, forced devaluations and interest rate cuts.[5] These are made in order to sustain public spending and the debts of governments and the bodies close

---

[5] See Ozihel, H. (2012) *Financial Repression*. Frac Press.

to them, be they banks or large corporations. They are policies that dip into the saver's pocket in order to finance the indebted. And investors defend themselves.

Why, then, do the media and politicians prefer not to disseminate or dwell more deeply on this positive aspect? Have you ever noticed that the press always say that "stocks and shares are falling due to pressure from the markets, or as a result of the situation in [insert foreign country]" or because of any other external excuse? Whereas when they rise, they say, "Stocks and shares have risen following successful intervention of the Treasury or after a few words from the prime minister." When everything goes badly, there is a need to point the finger at anyone save ourselves. We have to blame someone for the falls, and that someone should also be a good candidate for a measurable dose of conspiracy theory.

In 2008, it was widely decided that the "financial markets" were to blame, and it was certainly a brilliant idea for the following reasons:

- The phrase refers to something that is supposedly extremely powerful, an indispensable condition to be believable.
- It refers to something abstract, which is ingenious, as it cannot defend itself and thus cannot deny it.
- The guilty party is not in our country. This, in essence, is to lay the blame on people in other countries, which is always easier in a crisis. Historically, this has always been done: the best enemy is the foreigner.

Let's be serious. If several top operators convened every Monday in New York to decide which country to "attack" – I swear I have read this suspicion – they would be rather dimwitted. As much as anything, they would risk prosecution by the regulators for collusion, and would lose their business. If, by contrast, "they" attack without any justifiable reason, they will have an entire sector with an investment capacity of trillions of dollars against them, ready to make money by fighting back. This before central banks and their trillions of balance sheet capacity enter the arena.

The media forgets that the investors' own money and that of their clients is at stake, as well as their prestige, and that to bet on something that is known to be wrong from the outset is nonsense, when any bet is already a risk and subject to the volatility inherent to the market.

I won't forget the day when I was on a trip and suddenly received hundreds of emails and tweets on some statements made by a "mischievous" trader to the BBC in which he claimed to "dream about a crash".[6] In fact, many called him a broker, an alarming example of the ignorance regarding the responsibilities of each operator in the financial world. Twenty minutes after having listened to the interview on the BBC, I commented that it had all the hallmarks of a hoax... One hour later, we all knew that this man was neither a trader nor a broker, nor anything else, which says a lot about investigative journalism, as it takes only a minute to check online whether the man in question held an FCA (Financial Conduct Authority) or SEC (Securities Exchange Commission) licence to operate. However, the video went viral on the Internet.

What scared me at that moment, and what testifies to the obsession to demonise, is that once the hoax came to light, some voices argued that it was not important that it was a hoax, because in truth the message he conveyed was "What we all believe."

The magic phrase was "the market dreams of a recession" and no one was willing to stop believing in that conspiracy theory.

Why doesn't anyone in the market dream of a recession?

In a recession it doesn't matter who makes money: many market participants suffer dearly regardless. Nearly all of them. Well:

---

[6] http://www.bbc.co.uk/news/business-15059135

- In a time of recession, the money you make is relative. Bonuses are paid out in bank shares or deferred in the form of investment funds, thus the "evil speculator" feels the pinch the same as everyone else. Often the bank's shares plunge, making that "bonus" almost worthless, or the valuation of those investment funds falls dramatically. Thousands of people are indiscriminately laid off. If you keep your job you can count yourself lucky, but from there to becoming "filthy rich"... That's more the stuff of legend than reality.
- During a recession, the assets under management of investment funds drop sharply and indiscriminately because investors and pension investment funds seek refuge in cash.
- In a recession, banks and investment funds indiscriminately fire many of their workers, even the ones who are still making money, with the intention of obtaining a leaner organisation. As for the banks, they tend to eliminate their trading desks. Between 2008 and 2012, the City of London saw more than 150,000 people fired.
- In a period of recession, income from commissions crashes, both in terms of bank commissions and fund management fees.

No, almost no one benefits from a recession. Take, for example, the drop in assets under management in 2008.

An altogether different matter is when a difficult economic environment presents an opportunity to generate returns by taking refuge in low-risk assets – German government bonds, for example, non-invested cash or opening short positions. The market is an investment opportunity, not a donation. If the profitability expected from an investment is lower than inflation or the medium-term interest rates, it is not an investment; it is charity. As Charles Dickens said, "Charity begins at home."

The "dictatorship" of the market is an invention of countries and entities who have abused easy and cheap credit in the boom period and now expect the party to continue without paying more or changing a thing.

CHAPTER FIVE

THE LEHMAN CRISIS AND THE CHANGE IN MENTALITY: HABITS AND CUSTOMS

Thus far, I have described my first steps in finance, my motivations, my experiences and how I adapted myself to them. I felt it was important to debunk some of the myths and give my point of view on the media errors, and the mind-set of the operators and why they never really "attack". But we have still to examine the effects of the crisis on the people who work in the sector.

From the onset of the crisis until late 2012, $14 trillion were wiped off the value of assets. In all likelihood, this money never existed. The valuations that we held as adequate in 2007 were just justifications of bubbles created with the blessing and support of the central banks, which were pushing to take risks with their expansionist policies.

In 2007, the City of London employed 420,000 people. The total amount earmarked for bonuses awarded to executives, known as the bonus pool, topped £6.4 billion. That year my colleague Syman and others received offers from many investment funds. Syman always says, "I marked the peak". Indeed, the job offers that were received that year would never return.

In 2012, the bonus pool fell by 33%, according to the Centre for Economics & Business Research Ltd, and it was estimated that in 2013 it was worth £1.6 billion.[7]

ONS (Office for National Statistics) stats suggest the total bonus pool was £13.3 billion in 2012/13, almost exactly the same as the year before and down from a high of £19 billion in 2007/08, a 30% drop.

The workers of the City of London contributed £11 billion in taxes to the UK's Inland Revenue, seven per cent of the country's total revenue, and almost as many taxes as the whole of Scotland, for example, according to Ambition Consulting.

The City is a city within a city. It has its own governing bodies, which are coordinated between the mayor's office and the state. For many years it was – and remains – one of England's most important industries.

But life in the City is not easy. Many of its workers live far from the centre, some very far, 40 or 50 minutes by train, for example. Long working hours are the norm (at some banks they begin at six in the morning), as well as the tension, the competitiveness and the stress of living each year depending on your bonus.

It also places a strain on family life. There are women and men who give up their careers as doctors, pharmacists, executives, architects, even violoncellists from the Royal Opera House, because life in the City and public schools don't easily allow both spouses to work. Non-working parents devote their lives to picking up the children and then undertaking a marathon of extracurricular activities in the afternoons, because the good schools are also ultra-competitive. Children have to sit gruelling entrance examinations – some of which even I couldn't pass – for both prep and senior schools and are pushed hard to attain a stringent set of qualifications that form part of their

---

[7] http://tinyurl.com/ctdnnp6

preparation to join their country's ruling elite. The competition to get into some independent schools is fierce, and the children have to prepare themselves to pass an entrance exam where five hundred kids will compete for fifty or sixty places. All this requires private tuition, exam preparation and so forth.

This is how it is and everyone knows they are a privileged lot, but it comes at a high price and it is fraught with risk. It's not an easy ride. In fact, when I moved to the City in 2004, many colleagues survived from December to February, when the bonus is paid out, by living off their credit card or with the help of loans.

Naturally, when the good years come, they are extremely good. During the nineties and up to 2005, it was worth the sacrifice given the remote but not impossible prospect of buying a house with a one-year bonus, allowing oneself the luxury of purchasing a sports car or saving up to send the kids to Harvard.

The stress was enormous, but every one or two years one could afford to go on holiday to an exotic island location or something similar. Of course, some people made heaps of money. But many bonuses were paid out in shares of the banks where most of the operators worked.

Lehman Brothers and the banking disaster changed all this. It felt like a punch in the City's stomach, from which it still has not recovered.

Bloodbath in the workforce, zero bonuses and worsening working conditions have become commonplace. And they were real layoffs, announced ten days before Christmas and with little to no severance package. Three months' salary, in the best of cases, and then the street.

Many readers will think, "Well, big profits means big risks. I don't feel sorry for them", and so forth. Yet maybe they would change their mind if they knew the people who worked for twenty years as analysts, who never speculated, who never practised aggressive trading and who, at 45 years of age, found themselves jobless and without savings because they were fully invested in their banks' shares: Lehman Brothers workers, for example. They believed they had saved enough to last them the rest of their lives, and yet in a few days they had lost everything. I knew many of them.

When Lehman Brothers collapsed, the financial world realised that the warnings from many investors on the excessive debt of the banks were not "hedge fund fantasies", that the statements by Lehman's to the effect that "it was only the result of some naked short-selling attacks"[8] were wrong and that those who for years had been warning of the balance sheet and mortgage risk were not killjoys; they were right. Moreover, it became clear that the "Fed umbrella" (the Federal Reserve, the US central bank), the much-hyped and vaunted "safety net mechanisms by which central banks control the shocks" of which Alan Greenspan boasted, as do Ben Bernanke and Janet Yellen today, was a lie. It was not the collapse of Lehman Brothers itself that generated mistrust in the system but rather the arbitrary decision to bail out some banks and not others. On the other hand, as was demonstrated in Spain and other countries, bailouts sparked even more mistrust.

In an interview with *Sintetia* I said, "There is widespread concern that if a bank collapses it will bring the entire economic system down with it. This is only due to the huge interdependence between states and banks and vice versa. But this is not true. If an unsound bank fails, the sound ones are strengthened. By keeping them on life-support, it becomes impossible to differentiate the good ones from the bad ones, and this fuels mistrust. And there are great banks. We have seen this in the United States, in Iceland and in the countries of northern Europe."[9]

---

[8] http://tinyurl.com/cm29z4x

[9] http://tinyurl.com/c4owqfz

It's not easy to understand a bank's balance sheet. In fact, valuing the objective price of a bank's share is one of the most challenging things you can do, owing to its enormous complexity, the diversity of types of loans and businesses and the lack of detail in many areas. In my opinion, few people knew and understood better the complexities of the banks than a friend of mine, and one of the best managers I have met. Her name is Ann.

In 2006, she told me: "Daniel, I'm not sure where I'm going wrong, but every day, over and over again, I run an analysis of the banks [which at that time were rocketing] and I get valuations that are 70 to 75% lower." Ann had a bad year in 2006; she lost a lot of money. The usual: her banking valuations did not tally with the consensus. Ann, like so many others, could have been fired for having made a mistake in her analysis. However, her bosses were interested in this "anomalous" difference between her meticulous valuation and the market. What was the problem? According to her, the assets were not worth (at normal prices, which were already showing signs of saturation) that which was being accepted as correct, and nor was the debt of the banks adequate for the exposure that these shares showed.

In 2007, Ann's team was the only one that her bosses allowed to go "short only" (all short positions), as the rest of the teams had to aim for neutral or balanced portfolios. This huge bet was made possible thanks to the analysis of my prudent friend, who so scrupulously weighed up the fundamentals and the details. They earned hundreds of millions of dollars when the rug was pulled up, and the huge level of risk that many banks had been accumulating appeared below seemingly sound profit figures. She is now retired.

The day Lehman went bust, I left the office and, upon reaching Waterloo Station, noticed that almost everyone in the station or on the platform were City workers. The faces of those around me did not convey tiredness, but terror. The sight marked me. We had awakened from Greenspan's dream, that of the perpetual stimulus package, of low interest rates, exponential growth and the idea that "everything rises in the long term"; that of debt, banks and all that about how "traditional valuation serves no purpose for growing sectors". And that terrible awakening had caught many people "on the edge" and without lifejackets, as my friend Nacho would say.

The last days of Lehman have been widely documented in films and books like *Too Big to Fail*. I lived through those days.

The ruthless redundancies that followed created thousands of personal dramas. People who were operating in the markets from different positions, and most of whom had no part in the excesses of the decade of the free-for-all. Many of them lost all their savings because their bank shares crashed. Many others had to sell cars and watches to pay their children's school fees. The Bloomberg service has a function where workers of the City can put up for sale whatever they want. That year there were pages and pages of luxury cars at bargain prices and brand-name watches at derisory prices. Everything had to go.

The tough working regime in England and in the money markets in particular is unthinkable for someone used to the Spanish system. People arrived at work to find their access card did not work or that their personal belongings were in a box in reception. Or they found a makeshift tent erected in front of the bank through which they had to pass before entering the office, so they could be informed if they could get in or if they were fired.

The stock markets plummeted, commodities tumbled, bonuses fell.

The messages coming out of the media were that "it's only an adjustment period", "the foundations are sound", "companies see no need to revise their forecasts", "the valuations are extremely cheap", "the fundamentals have not changed", "it's a good company" and "it has good dividends". That year's great error was to try to find the market bottom and "benefit from the rebound", which is an incredibly dangerous strategy when the global macroeconomic context is changing so rapidly.

The rebound involved selling. Over $65 billion in assets controlled by investment funds were lost in one month when panic set in and clients decided to withdraw their money.

Obviously, there were some very good analysts who alerted people to the risks that the economic crisis would not be short-lived and that the fundamentals were not nearly as sound as they were made out to be, but most people paid no heed to these warnings. A huge number of managers, bankers, companies and private investors had made plenty of money on the rebound over the decade. Many had never experienced so profound a crisis, and it was difficult for them to see the warning signs of the scale of it all and the dangers of being overly optimistic. Investors were accustomed to the idea that things always fixed themselves in the end, and most believed that this was just one of those times. And the central banks were printing money and expanding the money supply. "Risk-on" mentality was not easy to change.

However, an economic model based on exponential debt began to collapse. There was no going back. Everything would be different. The solidarity between competitors was the feature that most surprised me of that black period. I thought that this was a world of sharks ready to let any competitor fall, and I found many people willing to help, to facilitate a job or even lend money to those who lost all their patrimony and found themselves without funds, for example, to pay their children's school fees.

Competition is fierce in the financial markets, yet at the same time no one wants to see the downfall of others, of countries or of companies – not even of competitors. We strive to be the best and earn more money, but a market needs "the others" to continue existing... otherwise, it would simply cease to be.

The debt crisis also led to the disappearance of the halo of confidence and certainty that surrounded governments and central banks, which did not stop them repeating that "the sovereign debt risk did not exist", that they had "provided for the eventuality of a financial meltdown" or, my favourite, that "The United States can pay any debt it has because we can always print money to do that. So there is zero probability of default" (Alan Greenspan).

Investors were beginning to pay close attention to those who had warned of the impending crisis, such as Peter Schiff and Ron Paul – the "spoilers" who had discovered that the Emperor was naked. Michael Lewis' book *The Big Short: Inside the Doomsday Machine*, became a best-seller. In my case, I went – via Peter Schiff, whom I met after reading his book *The Real Crash: America's Coming Bankruptcy* – to economists like Friedrich Hayek and his book *The Constitution of Liberty*, which defends freedom and warns against the excesses of interventionism.

In 2008, many friends and competitors lost their jobs and in some cases had to wait up to 18 months for a new opportunity. Few have forgotten the experience, and when they are told they are too pessimistic, that the recovery is coming, that the fundamentals have not changed or that things will improve in the long term, I'm certain that deep down they are thinking: "Sure, we heard the same thing in 2007." As they say in the United States: "Fool me once, shame on you; fool me twice, shame on me."

In 2014, we seem to be, again, at the top of a credit bubble. High-risk bonds trade at the lowest yields in thirty years, peripheral Europe government debt spreads have fallen to pre-crisis levels despite record deficits and debt, and emerging markets see countries issue debt at record low yields.

Easy money is not flowing to the real economy. Between 1996 and 2006, the largest companies in the US (which make up the S&P 500) invested about one trillion dollars per year, of which 70% was devoted to capital expenditure and R&D, while 30% went into buyback and dividends. Since 2009, the annual amount of total invested capital has soared to over $2.3 trillion, but 45% is used to buy back shares and pay dividends. In fact, neither the figure of productive investment nor R&D have increased substantially, inflation-adjusted, since 1998. That is, the "free" money from the expansionary policy is used for protection, reducing the number of outstanding shares, to merge and return cash to shareholders, not to expand organically.

The US has created nearly half of all the money supply of its history in the past five years, and has lived the longest period ever seen without raising interest rates. The balance sheet of the US Federal Reserve is rapidly approaching a staggering $4 trillion dollars, buying about a billion a year in bonds, yet the economy is growing well below its potential ... but also that potential is deteriorating. The risk of relying on easy money created from monetary expansion is too high.

Another symptom of the bubble of easy money is manifesting in the rapid sale of private equity stakes and the historical highs in exits and IPOs. Large investors who put tens of billions to work with the heat of low rates and monetary stimulus from the Federal Reserve are now retreating.

Buy well and sell better. That's the goal of any investor. Notice that I have not used the words *expensive* and *cheap*, wrongly used in the investor world, because those are concepts that are subjective and depend on the mood of market participants. Now we live in a period of euphoria and everything looks cheap. Well, when I started working in the City a colleague of mine told me, "Do not look at who is buying but who is selling." And now is when private equity and venture capital funds are selling more and better.

According to Brean Capital, 75% of companies taken public in the United States in 2013 traded below the IPO price in the first quarter of 2014, and 30% of them have been put on the market by private equity firms selling their stakes. The number of M&A (mergers and acquisitions) deals has reached a record so far in 2014. More than 4,880 operations, a total of $552.4 billion, back at the record levels of 2007, according to Dealogic.

There are positive indicators that deserve to be remembered. The global industry has entered an expansive phase for the first time since May 2012 and the indebtedness of European companies has fallen to 2007 levels. The private sector still works.

But these positive elements do not mask the fact that debt is growing faster than any indicator of GDP, corporate earnings, fiscal revenues or industrial growth.

The recovery still faces a very clear threat: the over-indulgence of debt accumulation just because cost is low, which leads us to the risk of spending a long time stuck at pedestrian growth levels.

The argument in favour of forgetting the debt problem is heard every day. It goes like this: What matters is growth. As long as economies get out of recession, and the cost of debt is low, governments should not worry, as little by little indebtedness will be reduced because the denominator, GDP, increases. All is fine. But it is not.

Expansive bubbles and easy credit always explode. Always.

A moderate investment environment will certainly have a further impact on countries accustomed to extreme liquidity. But it is essential to curb excessive credit fuelled by expansionary policies and to bring back investor sanity before this bubble is impossible to contain and brings unpredictable consequences, because crises, either through inflation, devaluation or financial repression, always end up being paid for by ordinary citizens

For the average stock market investor most of this is irrelevant. The worse, the better, and $85 billion of monthly asset purchases by the Federal Reserve, even if it is trimmed, makes everyone happy because the "helicopter money" only helps the financial sector and the indebted government, so we will "party like it's 1999" for a while. Furthermore, investors are protected by many companies who do not fall into the trap of easy money, because they are the first to suffer when the music stops.

I am sure that the innovative spirit of the US will prevail, but to estimate its economic development through the moves of a stock market affected by share repurchases and "cheap money" may be an illusion. Richard Koo warned that the US is engaged in "the QE trap" from which it cannot get out easily or comfortably.

CHAPTER SIX

TRADERS, "ROBOTS" AND SPECULATORS

In so competitive and stressful a world, there is also room for humour, to laugh at oneself and treat each other with irony. This is a pressure valve that helps us through the day. It's impossible to forget that the market is like the film *Groundhog Day* (Harold Ramis, 1993): everything you have achieved until yesterday doesn't matter, and every morning you start from scratch. One day, you may lose everything, and another day win. And then back to square one. Every second puts you to the test.

The media portrays a highly stereotyped image of investment fund managers, thanks to Hollywood movies like *Wall Street* (and its character Gordon Gekko) and *The Wolf of Wall Street*. Yet the reality is altogether different. Many managers are introverted people, slightly "nerdy", passionate about the markets and their inefficiencies, justified and unjustified. They do not question what is happening, and they know that the price and the result are the only yardsticks to differentiate a success from a failure. There is no place for excuses like "the market is wrong". The fund manager is wrong. There is no system more democratic, clear-cut, precise and Darwinian.

For me, having experienced corporate culture, which I also enjoyed immensely, the market offered an opportunity to test myself and to prove I could generate economic profits for clients. A harsh meritocracy also has its advantages if you enjoy the daily challenge.

The majority of the managers that I have met have a sarcastic and self-deprecatory sense of humour and a fighting spirit, hardened by many strokes of bad luck, blunders and also successes. We try to laugh at one another a little. I should admit that most of the criticism and ironic comments fall first on us.

Comments of the following type can be heard: "Why are the markets rising?" "Because this morning I made some negative predictions, it always works" or "Why are the markets falling?" "Someone has just come back from a round of golf and is selling" and "Because I bought this morning." When oil prices fall, someone will ironically comment: "Who was the one that wrote a bullish email?"

We also laugh at ourselves when we are having a bad day on the markets. I remember remarks such as: "Looks like my longs are going to bail out Greece" and "Right, with a capital increase." Or when announcements are made to bail out countries: "My portfolio is having a recession in my longs and bailing out my shorts."

One of the key things we learn is not to talk about "paper portfolios" (online portfolios where we include our best ideas to see how they would perform, but without investing real money) as they always work phenomenally. When we put them into practice with real money, however, many of these portfolios barely last three months. I have seen dozens of workers laid off who promised spectacular returns from their online portfolios. It's easy to handle Monopoly money, because there is no risk. It's another ball game altogether when you play with hard cash.

It's important to remember that we must not take ourselves too seriously and believe we are geniuses. There will always be someone much smarter, more sprightly and better prepared than you in another investment fund. Strong criticism from your own friends when success goes to your head, as well as their support when things are not going well, is essential to survival in this world.

"Robots" and how the markets are adapting to a changing environment

In 2014, Michael Lewis published a book called *Flash Boys*. It is about high-frequency trading (HFT) and it created quite a storm in the financial media and among various market participants.

Surprisingly, for how popular it is to vilify Wall Street, there are some interesting push backs to the argument. Part of the problem is that HFT means different things to different people. It is often confused with computer-based trading or algorithmic trading. Often it is spoken about in conspiratorial tones that make it sound illegal or something out of a bad Hollywood movie.

The biggest problem in demonising the impact of high-frequency traders in the financial market is that retail investors have benefited enormously in the last six years, with the S&P 500 at an all-time high in May 2014, making it hard to justify the claim that HFT "hurt small investors".

There are no special order types just for HFT, but there are many SEC-approved order types that are only used by the HFT type traders. It can cost upwards of $50 million to put the infrastructure in place that would make some of these order types useful.

High-frequency traders have a very low-risk tolerance so they fade any move (i.e. smooth out abrupt volatility changes). They don't stand still; they only transact when their model says they can get the offset. I am the same way, I only transact when I think it benefits me, but I think in 5- and 10-cent increments. HFT maths is done in fractions of a penny and includes rebates – my maths leads to finding other intuitions with different opinions or a different urgency on timing. Their maths leads to small trades with little valuation component – rather it is based on their ability to close out the trade at a profit or flat.

Mike Earlywine, a very experienced New York trader, made this basic HFT example:

Exchange A pays a few basis points if you take liquidity – business model promotes activity.

Exchange B pays a few basis points for posting trades – business model incentives providing liquidity.

Example

My super-fast computer sees that Exchange A has 100 ABC offered at $20.

HFT – step one – buy the 100 from exchange A get paid fractions of a penny on rebate.

HFT – step two – offer 100 shares of ABC on exchange B at the same price or a higher. price depending on my strategy and/or risk tolerance.

HFT – step three – hopefully someone buys those shares and I get paid again because exchange B pays for liquidity.

HFT – step four – repeat thousands of times a day in hundreds of different stocks.

Need for speed

Once I open a position, I need to get in the front of the book to post my closing position to reduce my risk exposure.

No free lunch: I am still exposed to the market and could lose money.

My models may have all kinds of stats on likelihood of execution but I still need to be the first to market to get paid.

I am competing not so much against traditional institutions but against other HFT players!

I have to compete to buy or sell the opening position and I have to compete to close it too.

Being late can expose me to market risk that my strategy is not designed to manage.

When I worked in the hedge fund world, they made us travel to the most out-of-the-way places, at any time and at very short notice, for the purpose of analysing companies better and acquainting ourselves with their managers. Having missed countless flights, wasted an outrageous amount of money and spent hours – sometimes days – in airports, we had some meetings with colleagues and decided to hire a private plane. At the end of the day, we covered the cost ourselves by deducting it from our bonus and, in an effort to save, despite having the right to a chauffeur, we negotiated the cities of the world by subway. The use of public transport gave one colleague more than a fright in the Moscow metro, and one foolish colleague who decided to take a bus in Johannesburg luckily escaped being kidnapped.

So I landed at New Jersey in a private jet accompanied by my three colleagues. "I bet I'm singled out for the 'random' search", my friend Sy always said. Sy was a doctor of computer engineering and a true genius. He was the creator of one of the most complete quantum models I have seen in my life, with over 300 macroeconomic and microeconomic data results to analyse trends. "I always get searched." Sy, being an Indian, had a dark complexion, and looked like a character from the film *Up the Creek*. A look very typical among hedge fund managers, even though it surprises people. The "outsider".

Sometimes, he would disappear for days and no one knew where he was. "Studying consumer trends at an Ikea store," he would say. "I've spent a whole day at McDonald's aggregating average spending." In fact, he devised an index based on the daily routine of a mother of two children in Chicago, which was a true revelation for analysing consumption habits. The fund tolerated his eccentricities, because he was a genius. Occasionally, he would go out for a drink at night. Those who went with Sy said that to accompany him one of those rare occasions was a guarantee of an epic evening worthy of John Belushi. But if you survived one, you would never do it again.

Indeed, every time we queued to pass through the metal detector, Sy would hear... "Excuse me, sir, random search."

Another colleague who was on the plane, Bellard, looked like an oil magnate. He alone took up two of the six seats. Clearly angry, he was reading reports and papers that he tossed into the air like the orchestra conductor in a *Bugs Bunny* cartoon, while the poor flight attendant picked up what she could. Meanwhile, I was reading an article on Renaissance Technologies, the investment fund belonging to Jim Simons, a mathematician who set it up in 1982 and in profitability out-performed all the world's managers, Warren Buffett included. Jim Simons once claimed "One can predict the course of a comet more easily than one can predict the course of a stock."

We had been asked to meet the managers of a mega hedge fund and a group of "high frequency traders". It sounded like a *James Bond* movie.

We had been working for some time on mathematical sys-tems and algorithms to try to "neutralise" the emotional factor and the white noise of personal or group perceptions in the investment process. Sy had spent entire nights tweaking mod-els, and we had a whole department given over to analysing the market from that perspective. Algorithms are not designed to cope with what happens in the stock market, and are not even based on what politicians do. They are designed to work out how securities will perform on the basis of published fig-ures; find the optimal combination of data that can make them rise or fall; analyse the numbers, both macroeconomic and those of companies, without forgetting to allow statistical esti-mates to move ahead of the results that other algorithms may provide, which in extremely accurate combinations generate a purchase or sale sign. It all seems very technical, yet it's very simple. Just as we analyse and forecast tidal movements or climate conditions, so we analyse the stock market by trying to eliminate irrelevant factors. And like climate prediction, the models can also be wrong. They are not infallible.

I have never applied this kind of mathematical methodology 100%, because in all the funds I have worked for the personal factor is highly valued, but of course the methodology is of immense help in questioning and revising your opinions. It's one more tool, and year by year it is increasing in relevance.

On that trip we were looking to learn and, rather than reject the invention of the wheel, try to understand it. The financial market is an ongoing adaption process. Complaining will only lead you to disappear, to become a dinosaur. It's futile to stand in the way of its momentum.

We were particularly interested in the use of "robots", or HFT, to carry out transactions on a massive scale and in the most efficient way. "HFT" refers to transactions conducted by mathematical algorithms at extremely high speeds: millions of trades are executed in very short times, usually in milliseconds. Of course, to this end HFT uses the fastest and most advanced software. After consolidating the ticker plants, the high-speed feeds are only 1.5 milliseconds faster than the regular ones, but that is enough for these guys to pick off stale quotes. (This is why co-location is so important. Every millisecond counts when you're stealing fractions of a penny.)

Today it is estimated that HFT algorithms account for a huge proportion of trading volume, almost 50%.[10]

The objective is to perform multiple transactions that yield a tiny return that gradually adds up.

Following the invention of the motorcar, hat makers were up in arms. Hats would fly off the heads of drivers or the

---

[10] http://www.forbes.com/sites/richardfinger/2013/09/30/high-frequency-trading-is-it-a-dark-force-against-ordinary-human-traders-and-investors/2/

drivers would be forced to hold on to them with one hand while driving, so they stopped using them. The hat manufacturers organised demonstrations and lodged complaints. In the same way that hat makers complained that the motorcar was the invention of the devil, there are those who hold that algorithms affect the stability and integrity of the markets. However, anyone who has used them knows that, like iPhone apps, each one is different and does not respond to the same inputs.

For us, algorithms are incredibly interesting given their neatness and in-depth analysis, and because they lower transaction costs, making it easier for investors to buy or sell when traditional investors prefer not to trade actively. Algorithms are not driven by emotional impulses, or by what Merkel or Bernanke says on a given day, and precisely for this reason, they are highly positive when unfounded panic sets in. This is usually sparked by the buyers.

Those visits were a revelation in many aspects, seeing those investment funds without hundreds of traders looking at screens and speaking to others, but just engineers, physicists and mathematicians analysing data, correlations and statistics. Not a single screen, no one listening to the latest statement by Bush or Bernanke or the CEB. I hadn't heard so many statistical terms, words like "multicollinearity" and "heteroscedasticity" since university. There, at those meetings, they cropped up several times.

We left those meetings like someone who has seen a Ferrari in a car showroom. Spellbound.

We were not going to do as the hat makers did, who saw their sales plummet after the invention of the motorcar. We had to learn and adapt. A few months after returning from that trip, we closed the private plane account. Of course, we continued making trips to Beijing to visit a car manufacturer, to Ghana to see an oilfield, but only when it was strictly necessary. White noise, wasting time and reducing hours of numbers analysis were kept to a minimum. No more trips to hear a company say what everyone already knew, attend an irrelevant presentation or see an asset that accounted for 2% of the company's value. Our travel expenses are now four times lower than in 2007.

The commodities and oil market

Peak oil is like a 200-million bonus: everyone talks about it but no one has seen it.

Trader's comment

Ron moved to Geneva having lived many years in London and tired of paying 55% income tax. He began his career as an analyst in a large American bank and, like me, he had gone from analysing oil companies and following the commodities markets to investing in them from a hedge fund. However, when the opportunity arose to join a major commodities trading house in Geneva he didn't hesitate. It would be a new experience in an industry as attractive as the commodities sector.

Ron and I met when he went into management. I was the client and he the analyst. His recommendation about an Italian refinery was one of the successes of 2006, and it made big bucks for both of us. Since then, we have been good friends and share a passion for the energy sector, a passion that is reflected in the analyses of the energy market I post in my personal blog, dlacalle.com.

When I moved to the oil industry in 1991, my best friend asked me: "Why? That's madness. Global output is at 60 million barrels a day and it's going to fall. There are barely enough reserves for 30 years; the industry is dead, according to *Newsweek*." In 2012, production reached 87 million barrels a day, proven reserves exceeded 30 years and available resources for more than 150 years were reported.

During my time in an oil company and as an investor, I have had the great fortune to travel the globe analysing wells and oil facilities first-hand, in countries from Sierra Leone, Ghana and Nigeria to Russia, Saudi Arabia, Iran, Venezuela, Colombia, Argentina, Brazil and so forth. The oil industry has changed considerably since the mid-nineties. A bodyguard would be sent to pick you up at the door of the plane at Abuja, Nigeria, to prevent you being kidnapped. We would travel in two cars in Colombia so that in the event of an attack on one you could jump into the other and try to make a getaway. At that time, when my colleagues told me how lucky I was to travel so much, I used to show them the safety recommendations of the Sheraton hotel in Ikeja, which I took with me as a memento. They advised you not to answer the phone and not to allow anyone into your room while you were inside, even if it was a member of the hotel staff, and never to accept an invitation to a meeting off the hotel premises.

However, I was also able to visit such wonders as the Canadian tar sand deposits, of which it was mistakenly said that they couldn't be exploited for less than $120 per barrel. I also gained in-depth knowledge of and invested in shale gas and shale oil (the 21st-century energy revolution) in Texas.

Fracking technology, thanks to the revolution of shale gas in the United States, is tried, tested and of negligible ecological impact. However, we have seen many alarmist reports, even a movie, *Gasland*, which was immediately refuted by the industry, scientists and the US Department of State of Energy as inaccurate... But best of all in these alarmist reports is that in every one you read that "we could not confirm accurately any of these claims" (the Cornell study, for example).[11]

Hydraulic fracturing technology is proven, is used in thousands of wells in the US annually safely and there have only been one or two cases of minor accidents. The fluids used in the fracking of the rock are composed of more than 99.98%

---

[11] http://dyson.cornell.edu/research/researchpdf/wp/2012/Cornell-Dyson-wp1212.pdf

of water (94.62%) and sand (5.24%), with a minimal amount of chemicals, highly diluted, easily stored and handled safely. Of these chemicals, the majority (hydrochloric acid, ethanol, methanol, ethylene and sodium hydroxide) are recovered perfectly in the extraction process. No state or local department in the US has found evidence of water pollution of aquifers. The industry is also using more than 5,000 tons of steel and cement to protect the groundwater, and the fracking process occurs at least a mile deep, well away from the aquifers.

This revolution has created $76 billion of GDP and 600,000 direct jobs in the US.

If you wish to know more about these revolutionary processes of fracturing rocks to extract gas and crude oil by using hydraulic pressure (commonly known as fracking), which according to the International Energy Agency (IEA) may allow the United States to overtake Saudi Arabia in oil production in 2030, I recommend you visit my blog in English (dlacalle.com). The industry's ability to grow and innovate, to discover vast fields like Jubilee or Tupi, has always held me in awe.

Since we first met, Ron and I have spent hours discussing oil companies, and together we have attended a fair number of OPEC (Organisation of the Petroleum Exporting Countries) meetings.

Vienna is a curious city. Peaceful, pleasant, clean and tidy. Incredibly expensive. However, from the moment you land and go through passport control, you are confronted with a series of huge advertisements, including some for shady-looking clubs, which are aimed at the select and wealthy group that meets there periodically: OPEC.

Each time there is a meeting, the airport receives scores of private planes and the city is flooded with limousines and sports cars. The hotels are filled to capacity and the huge retinues of delegates flock to the shops to buy luxury goods, clothes, watches, whatever. Then they depart, until the next meeting.

The OPEC meetings in Vienna are portrayed in the media like a reality TV show where everyone is squabbling. However, this is not true, and these are events worth attending. Although the press tends to mock the meetings as a high tea of ignorant oligarchs, the first thing that strikes you is actually the high level of expertise of the discussions. The second is the great deal of disunity among its members, not only between Venezuela–Algeria–Iran and the rest, but amongst all of them. This has intensified as disparities in the break-even price have increased between countries.

Delegates, princes and high-ranking representatives convene in a conference room. The media follows the meetings from another room and, in the meantime, the entourages are on hand in case the delegates need anything in particular. All the delegates address one another with exquisite diplomacy, even when they differ quite radically. No one raises their voice. Yet, to my mind, there are two voices that receive the most attention: Saudi Arabia and Iran, which, in addition to being poles apart in their policy towards the West, represent two very different conceptions of OPEC's supply strategy. Conciliatory and diplomatic (Saudi Arabia) versus the more aggressive and demanding (Iran).

When the press reports on OPEC, it tends to overlook the fact that the organisation is a cartel, an oligopoly, and it behaves as such when determining output. It's not the case that they cannot produce more than they do: indeed, OPEC always "cheats" on its quotas and produces extra. Instead, the organisation has a three-fold objective: ensure that demand can be met, guarantee minimum revenue for producers and provide appropriate returns for the industry (as is set out in their mission statement). Indeed, OPEC is not an NGO: it does not seek to show pessimists that it can produce more. Its objectives are economic. Many have acknowledged the mistake in assuming that Saudi Arabia was going into an irreversible decline in output.

Contrary to popular belief, the petroleum producers' behaviour is pro-cyclical, not counter-cyclical, meaning they increase output when the price falls to compensate for lost earnings, and reduce it to sufficient levels when the price is right. Hence, they meet as a cartel and set quotas to prevent episodes of excessive supply and demand shocks.

I learnt a good deal about commodities and how to analyse them from the traders of a firm based in Switzerland. After years of discussing whether there are enough oil reserves, if supply from one or another country is declining or not, the first thing I discovered was that demand and analysis are everything for the investor, as they are what really dictate price movements. I was beginning to grasp why OPEC had been so ineffective at controlling its prices.

The most challenging aspect for market operators has always been to assess which part of demand is real, as a large part depends on China (8.5 million barrels a day), which could push the "stop" button at any time if Beijing so decided. China, with a GDP of $6 trillion – compared with the United States' $14 trillion, and the EU's $16 trillion – consumes 53% of the world's cement, 47% of its coal and 10% of its petroleum. For the investor, the question is if these figures are sustainable. Hence Iran, Venezuela and Algeria, with a higher extraction cost (break-even $78–80/barrel), are consistently opposed to an increase in OPEC production quotas. If oil prices plunge, their economies would suffer more than those of the other OPEC members.

For the commodity investor, especially in crude petroleum, demand is a particular concern. And that's where the main focus of analysis is, above all because many investors persist in three arguments that never work in the medium term:

- Believing that the price of oil cannot fall because supply is running out and the producer countries need a high price to balance their budgets. This is an error of analysis the public often makes. It would be like saying that house prices had to rise 30% in Spain in order to put the banks back on a good footing. And if oil were to deplete, the marginal price would tend to zero because, logically, the last barrel of oil would have a zero price, since an alternative will have been found long before then, either by matching demand or by technology.

- Another myth is that the price of oil cannot fall because the marginal cost of Canada and other countries' production is $90–95/barrel. If demand doesn't rise, costly marginal production would disappear. Canada can lower its production, but it's not true that it would be as expensive as people assume, accordingly it is very difficult for it to drop below 1 million barrels a day, as we saw between 2008 and 2009. Russia and Saudi Arabia's production, with a marginal pre-tax cost below $50/barrel, would not drop from some 10 million barrels/day even with a 5% fall in demand (we have seen this).

- Lastly, there is not a single trader who believes in peak oil theory. This has already been challenged and criticised on many occasions, but even if you like these theories it's important to note that 2012 was the fourth consecutive year in which the petroleum sector replenished over 100% of its reserves. Furthermore, in the short term the system had 3 million barrels a day surplus capacity, the inventories of worldwide surpluses were above the levels of the last five years, and with the shale oil revolution, believers in peak oil theory, who have already revised the "disaster" date by several decades, will have to move it forward several hundred years more.

All analyses, therefore, centre on demand and on estimating how credible and sustainable projections are. In this respect, the demand projections of the IEA and other international bodies are not considered valid, because they are overly optimistic and because they collect data supplied by the countries themselves, which are always generous in their forecasts for growth and tend to underestimate the substitution effect and energy efficiency. To illustrate this, between 2001 and 2011 the United States saw a 6.3% growth in GDP while demand for gasoline and crude oil remained almost unchanged (+0.06%).

For a trader, demand is all that matters to maintain the price of crude and other commodities. So OPEC doesn't make a decision if economic recovery is not confirmed. OPEC, and the oil sector as a whole, often fears a disproportionate fall in price since the balancing of supply and demand is still very comfortable.

For a manager, there is no doubt that price movements in recent years are a result of the crazy policy of printing money, a.k.a. "quantitative easing" or "monetary expansion". The dollar has lost 95% of its value as a currency since the creation of the Federal Reserve. Quantitative easing since 1998 has been markedly aggressive: 20% in China, 30% Russia, and up to 6% annually in the Organisation for Economic Cooperation and Development (OECD). Analysing the price of oil indexed to gold, not to the dollar, we find that petroleum and other raw materials have not risen substantially since 2000. This period of massive destruction of the value of currencies by increasing the money supply is what best explains the alleged "rise" of prices of raw materials: we created artificial inflation.

When you visit one of the big trading houses in Switzerland, you realise two things: first, as we have already learnt in these chapters, that investors are not evil speculators who push up the prices of food and petroleum to make children suffer, but rather fundamental analysts that study the daily demand–supply balance of each one of these commodities, and whose influence on their price, according to scores of reports by the CFTC (United States Commodity Futures Trading Commission) is utterly insignificant.[12]

---

[12] http://tinyurl.com/bnmvcdj

Traders do not influence the price; they are agents who merely generate liquidity and would be happy to short commodities where demand is poor and there is oversupply, as happens with so many of them. In fact, they are essential for deflating bubbles caused by non-fundamental elements. And – surprise, surprise – another thing that we discovered is that they sometimes err: winning or losing. This is what the market is like.

Between 2005 and 2007, we also witnessed the renewable energy revolution. A trillion dollars was invested in new energies worldwide; an unusual boom stimulated by governments who unfortunately turned off the tap a few years later, leading to the collapse of half the industry. You can't trust governments. Another example of interventionism and bad planning that severely damaged many good companies. The RENIXX, which brings together publicly traded renewable energy companies, fell by 98% between 2008 and 2012. Another bubble of optimistic valuations, despite being a perfectly viable industry.

I had the opportunity to analyse and invest in large solar energy and wind power companies across the value chain. My activity was always limited to unlisted companies, because the valuations that we found when they went public largely seemed excessive. Having analysed conventional energy and worked in one of the funds which held the largest investments in renewables in Europe, I had a critical global perspective of all the segments, of the risk of excess capacity, of the subsidies and of the optimistic expectations. A spectacular experience.

PART II

THE DEBT CRISIS AND THE GREAT LIE OF FREE MONEY

CHAPTER SEVEN

THE DEBT MARKET

I learnt everything I know about the debt market from two people: Russell and Damien.

Russell bought and sold corporate and sovereign bonds. In 2004, he alone yielded half the returns of the investment fund where he worked. He was said to have earned $700 million in bonuses in the last three years. His bedside table book was *Bond Markets, Analysis and Strategies* by Frank J. Fabozzi.

If you met Russell in the street, you would probably offer him some small change for a cup of coffee. He is a dishevelled guy, with coke-bottle glasses that would make even Brad Pitt look ugly, and has a personal style that is reduced to "whatever he finds in the wardrobe". Shy, introverted, very likeable, Russell is an avid reader and a true expert in jazz. He is a multimillionaire, and yet he lives in rented accommodation, has no car and his one "indulgence" is to always travel by private plane on a NetJets account, as he never lives more than three months in any country. Since 2005, Russell had been warning of the spiralling debt that would put paid to many countries in the OECD. And it should be acknowledged that his behaviour was wholly consistent with his analysis.

Damien, by contrast, is an athletic type who looks after his image. He is passionate about windsurfing. Damien was a broker for a large investment bank in New York, and became a manager shortly before the sovereign debt crisis. While still a broker, he would listen to the bank's euphoric messages regarding the latest cut in interest rates, the latest stimulus plan and monetary expansion, and yet he only saw selling opportunities. So he left his quiet post and went into investment with several millions that some private investors loaned him. Damien predicted the sovereign debt crisis.

"Saying that a country's debt is not a risk is stupidity. It has the highest risk because it's paid for with taxes, cuts and less growth." Today, this message may seem obvious to you. I assure you that in 2004 it was not. Damien showed me that:

• The GDP-based ratios used to analyse a country's solvency are irrelevant, because GDP is a highly manipulated variable. For example, the GDP of Spain fell only 5% during the crisis until 2012, while all the other indicators of liquidity and solvency (revenue, industrial output, consumption, saving capacity, access to credit and so forth) fell by more than twice that amount.

Think of the "Chinese miracle". Prime Minister Li Keqiang, according to Reuters, referred to Chinese GDP as "man-made and for reference only". China continues to grow in a planned and superficially spectacular way. The machine is doing "okay" as long as the Government keeps it well oiled. It is the triumph of massive debt and central planning. Triumph? No, it is not. All this credit bubble would not be a problem if Chinese companies were making fabulous profits and margins were spectacular, which would make the debt easily payable. However, 48% of the Hang Seng Index (comprising the largest Chinese companies) generated returns below cost of capital in 2012 and almost 30% did not cover financial costs with free cash flow. Does that sound familiar to those who heard "debt does not matter because most is non-recourse" in peripheral Europe in 2007?

So what's the problem? The arguments supporting or justifying the Chinese model are:

- This is being a scaremonger. This has been the case since 2000.
- While there is credit available and the government decides it, China will grow as much as needed. There is no problem.
- As long as the non-performing loan risk is concentrated in its banks, there is no contagion to the rest of the world.
- There is no bubble, only a moderation of growth.
- As long as China grows above 5%, the rest of the world is fine.

Surprise, it's the same we heard in 2007–2008 in Ireland and Spain. However, China has huge implications for global credit markets, as it's the second-largest buyer of US Treasury bonds, and for the anaemic industrial recovery process on which Japan depends heavily to improve its exports.

- What matters for the fixed-income investor is the difference between revenue and expenditure, especially when expenditure is accelerating and revenue declining. It's as if you have a credit card and your income declines, you lose your bonus and your partner becomes unemployed, while your expenses are still neither rising nor falling. What happens first is that the cost of your card – the risk premium, the cost of debt – rises. Then, when things are no longer sustainable, your card is cancelled and you have to "restructure" (i.e. downsize and defer payments) for the rest of your life.

Damien told me back in 2007 that the risk premium would skyrocket. All liquidity indicators showed that high risk and unrestrained spending creates a vicious circle, akin to that of a family that lives on its credit card. At a time when this lifestyle was quite typical, there could be no better example.

Countries live much like those families that appear in TV ads and enthuse: "Consolidate your debts and bills into one convenient monthly payment and enjoy life." They stretch out the limit as much as possible in order to maintain a frankly unsustainable lifestyle. In short, they are mortgaging the future to justify reckless spending that, naturally, no one considers excessive.

"I've never lived beyond my means" is a remark repeated by companies, families and states, although it is often based on a generous and optimistic analysis of what "my means" actually were. The environment prevents us from understanding what our real means are, because for decades we have been given to believe we have a right to be increasingly indebted. Hence we hear, without batting an eyelid, statements from the Spanish autonomous regions to the effect that "we demand the same right to run up a deficit as the state" and "all we need is credit flow". Nor are we informed of the consequences and damaging effects of excessive debt, such as tax increases, cutbacks, runaway inflation and default risk.

Damien and Russell had something in common. They were able to decipher a balance sheet and discover the flaws or deliberate errors on an income statement in two minutes. They could analyse the real solvency of a country or a company in a few hours. Another thing they had in common was their refusal to be duped by promises of "long-term" and "green shoots", precisely because they were the type of investors who bought at even longer terms, with horizons of 5–10 years.

"The balance sheet, working capital and cash say it all, Daniel, and by reading balance sheets you will realise the world has gone mad." I inherited from Russell and Damien a passion for understanding financial statements. The boring numbers that many prefer not to see and others prefer us not to see. A bond investor is perhaps the most conservative of all investors across the market spectrum. After all, to buy a bond is to buy the debt of the state or a corporation in the hope that the risk attached to this financial instrument is low.

A bond generates profitability according to its coupon rate (interest) and, when there are more buyers than sellers, appreciation. Thus, they can be quoted "at par" (i.e. at 100, the pre-established principal amount), or with a premium or a discount. Bonds, therefore, are not always the low-risk opportunity we are led to believe. They may be quoted at a huge discount and generate losses despite paying out interest if the difference between their current value and received interest is high.

Bonds, T-bills, debentures, convertible bonds... What people cannot seem to get their heads round is that when a fixed-income instrument offers a disproportionately high return it is not a bargain. It simply means that it is an extremely high-risk product. Small investors – and many big ones as well – have spent decades hearing that fixed income entails no risk. It's false. Fixed income, sovereign bonds and corporate bonds entail risk, and the higher the debt, the greater the risk.

However, when Mrs Jones or Mr Smith asks the bank for a product which (since government bonds pay very little) will give them a good return, they are asking for a much riskier product without realising it.

I recall a relative telling me: "Look what's happened: I bought debentures convertible into shares because they offered a very good interest rate, and now I've lost 50% of the amount invested." The terms "debentures" and "convertible into shares" should have triggered alarms, knowing that the product was exposed to the fluctuation of the share of that bank when converted. A convertible debenture is, by definition, a capital increase, and as such it is a transaction that has a dilutive and possible negative impact on that bank's share price. But the investor and the issuer often prefer to look at their perception of "value", the supposedly attractive interest rate and the reassurance that "everything goes up in the long term" to justify a high-risk investment as if there were barely any risk involved.

The small investor and the selling bank tend to underestimate the risk of the underlying instrument (the principal; the invested capital), which is overshadowed by the promise of high "interest". The share price upon maturity is not valued in the case of a convertible debenture. Yet... why offer a high-interest return on this product? Out of generosity? A flight of fancy? Setting the interest rate of a fixed-income product is based precisely on an assessment process of the default risk or capital loss. The higher the rate of interest, the greater the risk perceived.

Naturally, you as an investor may decide that the profitability demanded by the market (the rate of interest) is too high and unjustified compared to the real risk, but if you draw this conclusion you should also consider whether this is an unsound view, or that it's based on the redundant traditional principles of "it's always been around" or "the bank manager told me".

Small investors also make huge errors on low-risk products. A fixed-income fund does not entail as much risk as a bond, because it's a different product. The fixed-income fund is more volatile and includes bonds as part of a portfolio. An American fixed-income fund is not the same as a Treasury bond, because the fund comprises many products with varying degrees of risk.

From the sell-side, be they governments, corporations or banks, these products are advertised as low risk, and the buyers and everyone else have accepted this pitch with far too much credulity. Perusing brochures, learning about risks and comparing them with the details of similar products and transactions is boring and tedious. Unfortunately, we often place too much trust in the seller or "expert", who sometimes finds these details and figures equally boring. They in turn count on another external source, or simply see the world from that optimistic standpoint that characterises us as human.

More interest, more risk. Please don't forget this.

Notwithstanding, this is a clear example of perverse incentives. For decades, states have been selling the idea that bonds are "risk free" to small investors. Since these investors associate "profitability" with interest rates, they forget the famous words of Will Rogers, a prestigious investor: "I am more worried about the return of my money, not the return on my money." It's not for nothing that high-yield bonds are called "junk bonds".

See how savers repeat themselves day after day: "How badly everything is going; the country has gone to the dogs", and then rush out to buy Treasury bonds because they offer a good "return". Their analysis of the world and their investment decisions are grating. Either they don't believe everything has gone to the dogs or they are wrong in their perception of investment risk.

We can regulate ad nauseam. Without financial literacy, however, financial instruments will continue to look like scams. It's essential that the public become financially literate. Instead of complaining posteriorly that "this was recommended to me", the best cure for ignorance is information: to learn and especially to realise that the markets are not to blame but the people who don't know how to control their impulses. They allow themselves to be advised by people who probably have as little idea as they do, or they let themselves be carried away by beliefs, such as "it's always been around", that have been perpetuated over the years.

Better to be safe than sorry. If there is something you don't understand, like a product that does not clearly display its contents or ingredients, don't buy it. Even if it comes in brightly coloured packaging and is offered by an attractive and friendly man or woman. Let me repeat: the higher the interest, the greater the risk. If you decide that that risk is overstated or misunderstood or that it will do better in the long run, that's your decision.

All the regulation in the world will not compensate for knowledge and common sense. It all boils down to finding out and learning. It's no fun, yet it's the only way. And even then we may still get it wrong.

> *Zero rates for countries that spend more than they earn. Sure it'll work.*
>
> Trader's comment

While states, companies and the media were talking about debt all day long and putting across the idea that the top priority was to keep interest rates down and announce never-ending bailouts, a new bubble was created: the bond bubble. As Warren Buffett put it: "Right now, bonds should come with a warning label." Successive liquidity injections and state bailouts took sovereign bonds, not least American and German ones, to an unacceptable level of profitability compared with the risk. This was also true of corporate bonds, above all junk bonds, now inappropriately called "high-yield bonds" because the term hides their risk.

Buying bonds whose intrinsic risk is underestimated owing to interventionist pressure is potentially far more hazardous than it seems, because the real risk is disguised. State action bent on creating inflation and injecting liquidity promotes a bubble on either side of the risk: "low-risk" US and German sovereign bonds on the one side and corporate high-risk bonds on the other. That zero-percentage interest rate on American or German bonds is as unjustifiable as receiving only an 8% coupon rate on bonds issued by corporations on the verge of collapse.

The first rule of capitalism states that individuals are free to invest their money where they see fit and accept the corresponding risk. The risk of bankruptcy and losing everything is essential for the smooth running of the free market. The good manager is rewarded, and the risks of a bad investment are clearly established. However, when bailouts come into the game, the principle of debt responsibility is destroyed. Bailout pledges give rise to perverse incentives and exaggerated risk-taking, and lead to the collapse of the entire system of credibility.

CHAPTER EIGHT

WELCOME, INVESTORS!

Europe has no problem with debt. Debt has a problem with Europe.

Trader's comment

In 2006, Toby (the person who hired me), Russell and I travelled to Spain to visit the government and some companies in the construction, infrastructure and energy sectors. Spain was in the spotlight at the time, following a spate of mergers and acquisitions made at extremely high valuations and paid for with debt, the construction boom and huge public spending on infrastructure.

We arrived at a large construction company, where the investor relations manager told us that the president would not receive us. "There's little point in seeing the President if you're here to speak about debt reduction, because that's not the value creation model of this company."

Other empty talk we heard on that trip included: "House prices in Spain can only go up because immigrants have lots of children and they will have to purchase", "There is no subprime crisis in Spain because the last thing people stop paying is their mortgage", "There are no subprime mortgages in Spain because there is no labour insecurity like in your country [the United States]" and my favourite, uttered by a senior member of the Spanish government: "You're jealous of the Spanish model." "But I'm Spanish" I replied. "Indeed, but you are contaminated by these two", – referring to Toby and Russell. The meetings were extraordinarily surreal, because the one thing these messages indicated was that debt was clouding everything.

In a conversation with the CEO of a construction firm who said that apartments in Spain should converge at €3,000 per square metre in all the big cities, Russell enquired if he had worked out how many years it would take an immigrant couple on two incomes to pay this price increase. He replied, "No, I haven't calculated it." "Ninety-five years, more or less," said Russell. "That's what you would say. I have nothing else to discuss." And he showed us the door. If the American mortgage crisis was the "big bubble", we had just discovered the "steroid-bloated sister of the big bubble".

Since then, when I began writing for the press and collaborating with the mass media, my aim has been to divulge the basic concepts of economics and finance. My goal is to share with the public my experiences and opinions, as well as my market and macroeconomic analysis.

CHAPTER NINE

THE EUROPEAN AND SOVEREIGN DEBT CRISES

I will never forget one day in 2008 when, in the midst of the crisis, we were watching a debate on TV in which the Spanish prime minister was speaking of the need to increase the budget deficit and place the country in debt with stimulus policies. My son Jaime, who was six at the time, asked me what was happening. I told him, "The government has seen the country is not working properly and he thinks that by spending more things will get better". My son asked, "Does the president have a lot of money?" "No," I replied. "He has to borrow it." Jaime looked at me and said: "So if he doesn't have money, how will he spend more? What a silly-billy he is." And off he went to play.

My three children, like all children born into the decade of extravagance, which spans 2001 to 2011, came into the world unaware (like everyone else) that thanks to the selfish deficit policy, wasteful spending and debt they were inheriting a debt of €27,000 each.

Let me give you a figure: €3.4 trillion, 3,400,000,000,000 euros. This is the debt that the eurozone countries ran up between 2006 and 2011. Three times Spain's GDP.

More debt in five years than that amassed in the period of time from the creation of the euro until 2006. And pulling the rug from under Greece was all that was needed to discover that the emperor was naked and the ability to service that debt had been unsustainable. Next came Portugal and Ireland, followed by Spain and Italy.

I heard again a sentence that tends to be repeated frequently: "Deficits support growth." It assumes that increasing deficits helps economic recovery, rather than that such a recovery is much slower and more fragile precisely because of the large deficits and the cost of financing them with taxes.

The nascent recovery we see in 2012–14 has a very clear threat: the over-indulgence of debt accumulation – the saturation threshold, destructive debt and the volatile cost of debt.

- **What is the threshold of debt saturation?** The point at which an additional unit of debt does not generate economic growth, but simply stagnates the economy further. This threshold was surpassed in the OECD, between 2005 and 2007.
- **What is destructive debt?** It is the debt generated by unproductive current expenditure, which produces no positive effect on growth and perpetuates a system that confines and engulfs the real economy through taxes, detracting investment and annihilating consumption. In the EU or the US, that would be a structural deficit of nearly 4% of GDP.
- **The volatile cost of debt.** What makes us think that bond yield and cost of debt are going to stay low forever? Bond yields cannot be kept artificially low forever. And that's when we see debt shocks, because the outstanding debt accumulation increases while low yields are unsustainable.

"Cheap" public debt is not a free pass to spend. In fact "cheap" is a misnomer, since it assumes that there is no cost of opportunity in private investing or saving.

Cheap debt is dangerous. Think of the perverse situation in a country like Japan, with a debt of over 200% of GDP, where the country's financing needs are over 60% of GDP in 2013. Its ten-year bond yields only 0.7%, so the country's incentive to reform is very low because debt is cheap, yet if there is an increase in the yield of 100 basis points it would endanger the entire economy. Japanese public debt, cheap or expensive, is more than 24 times the country's fiscal revenues.

Between 2008 and 2013, according to Deutsche Bank, the G-7 countries have added almost $18 trillion of debt to a record $140 trillion, with nearly $5 trillion from central banks' balance sheet expansion, to generate only a trillion dollars of nominal GDP.

That is, in the past five years, to generate a single dollar of growth we have "spent" $18 – 30% from central banks – while maintaining the system's total consolidated debt at 440% of GDP.

This "investment" in growth that is supposed to be accomplished through astronomical deficits, debt and the aggressive expansion of central banks simply does not bear fruit. Of course, many say that the solution is to continue doing it until it works. But the system becomes increasingly fragile and subject to massive shocks with the slightest movement of interest rates.

These pedestrian growth levels also occur in the middle of a fierce financial repression period. Devaluations and interest rate cuts discourage savings, and push the system further into debt. Money is "cheap" and saving is considered "silly". But meanwhile taxes are raised and disposable income is destroyed.

It impoverishes the population in four areas: savings, their profitability, real income and consumption capacity.

This leads to a much weaker system, because the fixed costs (i.e. public spending) multiply in cyclical economies, leaving very little room for manoeuvre in hard times. And then governments say it is a revenue problem, as if a country's public expenditures can be planned expecting the bubble to return.

George Osborne, in the UK, said: "A government that spends £720 billion a year cannot be called a government or an administrator, it is unacceptable." Notice he did not say in a moment "it is a revenue problem", which is what we hear in Europe all the time. Revenues come with economic activity, and if we suppress it through taxation to finance unacceptable expenditure this economic activity will not improve.

> *We all know what to do. We just don't know how to get re-elected after we've done it.*
>
> Attributed to Jean-Claude Juncker

The onset of the crisis was not the fault of one party or another, or of the banks or American mortgages. The crisis began when we began to believe that money was free, when the deluge of European funds had to be spent fast and uncontrollably so we would receive more. It was this perception of free money that brought us to the current situation, in which the masses rebel and demand more public spending (debt), more deficit (debt) and more subsidies (debt). It's a Europe-wide problem for all the OECD and in particular for the peripheral countries. Spain was a clear case of delusions of growth.

Wishful thinking that Spain would experience boundless growth can be found in (so-called conservative) predictions by the autonomous communities, banks, companies, regulators and the mass media during the first half of the nineties, but not least in the years of lost opportunity – 2004 to 2011 – when we made every effort to hide the problems of our economic model and the bursting of the housing bubble. Instead of putting out the fire, we poured petrol on it with more debt. You will recall these words by the then-Spanish prime minister, José Luis Rodríguez Zapatero, as the crisis was unfolding:

"We'll overtake Germany in per capita income. From now until 2010, we can perfectly well surpass them. First match and then slightly surpass them. Growth in Spain is at 4%. And we will create employment. With just this one figure, as president of the government, I feel completely at ease with our performance.

"We have the lowest unemployment rate in our history. Spain's economic model is an international model of solvency and efficiency.

"The crisis is a fallacy, pure alarmism. We are growing at above 3%. Even if tomorrow we grow at 3% or at 2.8%, which is still good growth, we'll continue creating jobs and enjoy a surplus."

The debt burden threshold seemed not to exist in Spain. But we easily surpassed it in less than two years.

The belief, still widespread, that the long term justifies everything, clouded Spain's investment decisions. It didn't matter. Conservative criteria and detailed planning disappeared to make way for the need to spend anyhow and as soon as possible. "If you don't use up your budget, next year you'll get less" is a phrase often heard in public and private entities.

Access to credit was assumed to be unlimited, so much so that even today we expect "flowing credit" as a condition for recovery. Few talk about profitability, improving margins, setting up companies without the need to indebt them by two or three times the value of their assets.

We have created a society addicted to debt, and one which equates debt with growth and spending with investment. Only aggressive therapy can cure us of this addiction, because half-measures have dug us deeper into a hole from which it will take a long time to climb out.

How did the perception that debt doesn't matter come about?

It stems from the mantra that "sovereign debt entails no risk" and that "public spending is an investment that can be recovered in the long term", hence the colossal error of analysis across all sectors. This belief underestimates the country risk which, interestingly, was also underestimated when assessing our multibillion-dollar investments in Latin America.

Imagine that the low-yield party continues, and the "Japanisation" of European economies deepens. If we, as Japan did, absorb the vast majority of our debt, we will be able to deceive ourselves by artificially lowering the cost of borrowing to an unacceptable level (such as the 0.7% of the Japanese ten-year bond). But what will happen? We will have created the perverse incentive to increase spending, not reform the economy, and so make debt shoot up to 220% of GDP, and this will be too tempting to be ignored by any government. And then the problems will become insurmountable, because European economies don't have the same high levels of citizens savings rate, productivity, exports and leading industries as Japan.

But imagine that this debt accumulation "does not matter" because we're putting it in our pension plans and our investment funds and it finances our airports, highways, hospitals, schools. It's the social contract, right? The only contract signed by the unborn to pay for the privileges of the living.

The problem is that such social contracts sweep away disposable income and savings in financial repression and taxes to finance public expenditure. In the EU, it exceeds 45% of GDP.

The absolute costs go up because it is always deemed as "little", and the unit costs also soar because the population ages and fewer taxpayers contribute to that imaginary contract. So the economy stagnates. Debt grows. And one day, everything explodes. By then, economists will say that the solution is a devaluation or a debt-haircut, which is to impoverish the entire nation again, destroying its pension funds and savings.

How could this have happened?

For years, we were told that capital was virtually unlimited. Optimistic forecasts became not only an excuse for barely justifiable malinvestment and public and private spending but also almost a religion.

The obsession of many politicians, to cite Paul Krugman or Joseph Stiglitz, two laureates of the Nobel Memorial Prize in Economic Sciences, is by no means coincidental. Politicians take the messages that interest them from these experts. "More public expenditure to stimulate domestic demand, and forget the deficit." Who doesn't like to spend more? Even citizens applaud this. Another useless airport, another stimulus package.

It's like telling a child to eat more sweets or an alcoholic to drink more. They are messages that appeal to the state's overprotective role and to our snug, selfish and wasteful side. Then, when these policies don't work and the country experiences runaway debt, as happened in Spain and Argentina, the person on the street or future generations suffer the consequences.

The IMF (International Monetary Fund) showed that, if we compensate for the effect of debt, Spain has hardly grown in the last decade. Therefore, people should rethink the messages that spending should be increased. Resolving debt with more debt will only exacerbate the disaster. We forget that when we pay for current expenditure with borrowed money, our children will foot the bill, plus interest.

There is nothing unconventional about monetary stimulus. It has been implemented over and over since the days of the Roman Empire. Take the policy implemented by Japan to fight deflation called "Abenomics". It is nothing new, just bigger. The country has made tremendous stimulus plans since the mid-nineties and expansionary policies since 2001 without exiting stagnation. It is curious that the monetarist policies are defended as being social and redistributive. However, there is nothing social in printing money. The Swiss investor Marc Faber explained it clearly in his *Gloom, Boom and Doom Report*: "Printing money does not benefit anyone other than those who have access to such funds, i.e., the financial sector, the government and the upper classes, never the workers."

A year after the implementation of Abenomics we can check some of the mistakes used to justify these measures:

PRINTING MONEY GENERATES MAGIC GROWTH

The Japanese economy grew 1% annualised in the fourth quarter, compared with 2.8% expected, and not enough to offset the slowdown in the third quarter.

In 2014, the IMF estimated that Japan's economy would grow by 1.7%, and the eurozone's by 1.1%. That is, with the Bank of Japan increasing the money supply at massive levels, the IMF expects very modest growth, while in Europe a similar GDP growth is generated when the ECB reduced its balance sheet by 20%.

PRINTING MONEY REDUCES DEBT

It just doesn't reduce the pace of growth in debt. Increasing the money supply more than the United States, Japan's public debt reached a record volume of 1,018 trillion yen in December 2013. About €7.3 trillion after six stimulus plans since the nineties.

The amount exceeds the 1,011 trillion yen of September and is more than twice the nominal GDP. Debt grows not only in absolute terms but also relative to GDP. All I hear is, "We must give it some time" … after only 25 years of Keynesian experiment, it "was not enough".

Printing not only increases the total debt but also increases the trade deficit to an unacceptable level. Some try to justify this with reference to the effect of the Fukushima accident and the cost to rebuild Tohoku after the earthquake. But it's the typical Keynesian excuse when something does not work. Tohoku has an annual cost of 1 trillion yen (2013) and the trade deficit exceeds 11.4 trillion yen, the biggest hole since 1979.

Fukushima and the closure of nuclear power plants was a single event in March 2011, and until Abenomics was implemented the trade deficit was manageable. Since then, it has tripled. Devaluing makes the cost of imports skyrocket more than the placebo effect of exporting more.

PRINTING MONEY COMBATS DEFLATION

Here comes the trick of adding figures. Proponents of monetarist policy to "create inflation" are very happy because in May 2014 Japan reached 1.6% and is on track to reach the government's target of 2%. Remember "inflation is taxation without legislation" (Milton Friedman). The silent tax. But there's a trick. Inflation in Japan rises because of energy costs and imported goods, not because wages grow or we see an improvement in other factors. In fact, inflation, excluding food and energy, is very low, just 0.7%.

The belief "if inflation is generated, the Japanese will consume more" has yet to be proved. It does not encourage consumption or economic activity acceleration because disposable income and wages are curtailed. Before the expected sales tax in 2014, the disposable income and purchasing power of the population suffered greatly. Real wages in Japan fell to their lowest level for twenty years. Money flowed only to risky assets. On top, the stock market rebound was irrelevant to the wealth of the Japanese, who had less than 8.5% of their financial assets in equities, compared with 32.7% in the US…

PRINTING MONEY CREATES JOBS

Japan has always had very low unemployment. Not because of monetary policy, but because of demographics. An unemployment rate of 3.7% is due to a spectacular industrial power and business climate, and a culture of work and sacrifice recognised worldwide... And an important demographic effect. Since the 2007 highs, with 128 million inhabitants, the population has fallen at a rate of nearly one million annually. In 2013, there were 244,000 fewer than the year before. This has created a shortage of work... and a brutal surplus of pensioners (23% of the population is over 65 years) at a cost to the state that the Japanese government considers "unaffordable".

Printing money does not create jobs. Otherwise, the countries that do it would have had full employment for years. But it's still worth noting that the labour participation rate in Japan has also plummeted, rebounding slightly when real wages have collapsed, especially for women, to 1994 levels. Japan, unlike the United States, has a shortage of workers owing to the effect of the low birth rate (1.4 children per woman) and an ageing population. And yet, if we remove the pensioners effect, nearly 17 million people of working age have been taken "out of the charts" of unemployment.

When Abenomics finally ends up generating pedestrian growth, more debt and lower real salaries for citizens, some will defend the money printing policy saying, "It could have been worse", "Not enough was done" and "We need to repeat it." And mistakes will be supported by a social veil that neither you nor the Japanese people will see. Then we will read, "We have to be patient; improvement comes next year," while the average citizen feels another hand in their pocket.

Of course, there is a solution. Return to moderation, to what made the Western economies a model not of debt but of the creation of well-managed and little-indebted businesses. Curtail political party spending and rethink a risk-adequate view of profitability. I will expand on my proposals in a later chapter.

However, when there is no will to implement painful domestic solutions, external culprits are sought.

CHAPTER TEN

CREDIT-RATING AGENCIES

Since the beginning of the economic downturn, a trillion dollars has been lost worldwide in purportedly "low-risk" triple-A-rated assets. The loss of the top credit rating by countries and corporations simply deters many investors from buying their bonds. However, despite the loss of the highest rating, some countries and companies, rather than reduce their debt, continued to increase it. A smaller-size "cake" of available capital, but with more diners trying to grab a big slice.

The first reaction to the subprime mortgage crisis in the United States was to set in motion the machinery to seek out external culprits: the only mechanism that has worked properly during this decade. Thus the finger was pointed at the credit-rating agencies, who were charged with evaluating sovereign and corporate rankings and issuing "grades" within a number of valuation ranges that chiefly fell into two: investment grade or non-investment grade, also called "junk".

Within this blame game, we once again forget how the market works and how the credit-rating agencies follow the equity analysts, who carry out their valuations from a perspective which tends to be sunny, diplomatic and generous to companies. Yes, the rating agencies have been hugely inaccurate, but they have always erred on the side of optimism, and rarely (I don't know of a single case) of pessimism.

I always say that a credit rating agency is like an entity that charges Paul McCartney and Yoko Ono a fee for telling them that the Beatles are going to split up.

My friend Jeremy is an analyst for a credit-rating agency. It's neither easy nor pleasant work. Rating analysts don't earn high salaries, and they are under constant pressure from governments and corporations to improve their ratings. Always. Every country feels it has an acquired right to be passed. Just like companies with buy recommendations. The pressure from the sellers is tremendous: "They don't understand us" and "They don't value our potential." Every time an agency downgrades a rating, albeit a technical one, it receives more calls from ministers and threats from secretaries of state than anyone else. No, it's not an easy job. The states and corporations themselves provide the agencies with their own data, which by definition is already much massaged. And when my friend uses his own predictions, he suffers the wrath of all the issuers.

"I'll fix it" was a typical remark from the president of a country when an agency announced it was going to downgrade that country's credit rating.

Diplomacy is so disagreeable. Throughout the entire crisis until 2008, the European countries, regions and corporations boasted about their "excellent credit rating" despite the fact that the prophets of doom, the unpatriotic and the evil speculators (like me), were arguing that things were going seriously wrong. And in the nanosecond in which the agencies finally, in the face of all the empirical evidence of the crisis, began to lower the ratings to the levels that the market had already accepted... came the outrage.

It was just like when we were young and we would say, "I got bad marks because my teacher has it in for me." The delirium came when we heard some members of the EU threatening to ban the credit-rating agencies from publishing on the eurozone countries. A childish tantrum. Since the EU states were unable to reach an agreement on how to resolve the debt crisis, they resorted to populism.

The rating agencies can be justifiably criticised for many things, save "attacking" Europe. In fact, they should receive great criticism for being too diplomatic with countries and reacting only when the warning signs of risk are evident, not before. Hence, what the market already saw in 2006 did not materialise in the credit ratings until 2009/10. Standard & Poor, Moody's and Fitch have been extremely benign. This is because they can only use documented data, and never make predictions that differ radically from the issuers' data. This also explains the agencies' tardy reaction to the subprime crisis.

And let's not fool ourselves: the issuers are perfectly aware of the real credit difficulties. But their keenness to publish them is another matter.

We are told that credit-rating agencies have a short-term outlook and an Anglo-Saxon animus against Europe (though Fitch is actually based in France). It's an absurd accusation, bearing in mind that they have always published ratings based on the forecasts provided by the countries themselves (and which, naturally, were not met). A little self-awareness wouldn't go amiss.

In reality, investors value the work of the agencies less for their credit rating than for their in-depth analysis. Their recommendations are no longer followed as they were prior to the subprime crisis, yet they continue to give plenty of value to the content, and independent agencies like Egan-Jones are being used increasingly more.

Interventionists call for a ban on credit-rating agencies' publishing reports on the eurozone. What nonsense. Let's see how the refinancing processes of European corporations would fare if the investors who had to buy that debt had no access to an accepted considered state rating. But of course, politicians are not interested in the refinancing of corporations, only public debt, which is sustaining their exorbitant spending. They prefer their countries to go bust.

Others hold there should be more competition between rating agencies. Good, but be careful what you wish for. What if agencies emerge like Egan-Jones or Weiss Rating in the US that tell things exactly as they are and highlight the true nature of our national debt? These agencies estimate that the true credit rating of the United States or Europe would be closer to C than A. Others say there should be a European credit-rating agency that analyses data from a "close" perspective. Close. In other words, someone who says what our politicians want to hear. As if investors would lend credence to "advertisement analysis". I call such a proposal the "LOGSE rating agency", where everyone passes despite destroying the balance sheet.[13] Little credibility would be given to a body that further mires the image of the diplomacy and caution of the current rating agencies.

Some time ago, I spoke to the director of one of the few companies that conduct analyses focused exclusively on the balance sheet. He agreed with me that we have spent too many years blinded by the fantasy of debt over GDP, when cash flow and the weight of debt on revenue are what really count.

Europe and Spain must stop burying their heads in the sand and waiting for everything to clear up, and instead focus on regaining their credibility so as to attract capital instead of scaring it off. They must stop living in the fantasy world of politically motivated spending, easy credit, the stupid subsidy gravy train and the acquired rights that we deny to others. Then they will see there is no need to ban and intervene. Demand will come by itself.

---

[13] Translator's note: LOGSE, a controversial education law passed in Spain that automatically passed underperforming primary school pupils, allowing them to proceed to the next grade. These pupils' failure to acquire basic skills subsequently led to a high dropout rate in the secondary education system.

CHAPTER ELEVEN

WHEN THE PROBLEM ONLY SEEMED TO BE GREECE

Portugal is not Greece. Spain is not Greece ...
Greece is not Greece.

Trader's comment

In November 2012, the Eurogroup and the IMF decided to release a "further" €43 billion so that Greece could honour its payments. In terms of bailouts, Greece has received a sum amounting to ten Marshall Plans between the start of the economic crisis and late 2012. However, all that has been achieved in the last few years to solve unsustainable debt issue has been to "kick the can down the road".

According to Reuters, in January 2013 unemployment rose to 26.8% – the highest rate in the EU. In December, the Greek parliament passed the 2014 Budget, which was predicated on a return to growth after six years of recession. Prime Minister Samaras hailed this as the first decisive step towards exiting the bailout.

However, the Greek government's forecast of a return to growth was at variance with the predictions of the OECD, which forecasted a 0.4% contraction of the Greek economy in 2014.

Whether by bailouts or by default, Greece has highlighted Europe's vulnerability and the risk of "solving debt with more debt". Greece was not the problem; it was just one link in the problem, but it showed us the extent of destruction that such a small country can cause to the global financial system (owing to other countries' exposure to Greek debt).

Meanwhile, the only things that have remained unchanged in Greece are the over-bloated state bureaucracy, political spending and cronyism within the public administration and political parties. I recommend you read the chapter given over to Greece in *Boomerang: Travels in the New Third World*, by Michael Lewis, in order to understand why we will never again see the money we loaned it, and why keeping a moribund state in a euro that it really cannot afford is good for neither Greece nor the European Union. It's only beneficial for the banks, particularly the German and French banks, which amassed €138 billion in Greek debt in 2011. Meanwhile, Greece's debt as a percentage of GDP soared to 175% in 2013, according to Eurostat.

In response to this snowballing debt, the European Central Bank has provided huge injections of capital, which generated considerable risk. Since most of this liquidity was used to allow the banks to buy sovereign debt, it gave rise to a vicious circle. On one hand, the liquidity did not reach the domestic-based economy (loans to families and businesses continued to fall) and on the other, risk was doubled (the balance sheets of the banks and public debt together). When the state's risk premium was rising, the sovereign bond portfolio of the banks became an unacceptable risk.

However, Greece was not the problem. At least not the only one. The economic crisis had been brewing across Europe for many years. The loss of private capital and the de-industrialisation of the Continent were compensated for by more public and politically motivated spending, which, rather than generate positive marginal returns, only created more debt. In addition to spiralling unproductive expenditure, Europe embarked on a phase of government interventionism and a tax revenue baccha-nalia through new taxes that sparked foreign capital flight and the acceleration of the de-industrialisation of the eurozone.

The United States and the United Kingdom initially began to resolve the economic crisis with private investment funding, capital injections, mergers and acquisitions: incentivising the industrial sector to invest, restructure and regain efficiency, while deleveraging the financial sector. In Europe, the economic crisis and de-industrialisations were disguised for as long as possible with bank debt. Interventionism and protectionism were resorted to in order to avoid having to spring-clean the industrial sector. Inefficient companies were merged (with the blessing of governments) to create giants that were even more inoperative. Low-productivity sectors were shielded to avoid the necessity for restructuring or the inflow of foreign capital. Eve-rything was financed by banks with close links to states that were seeing their balance sheets grow at an alarming rate. "If the government requests credit, you don't analyse it, you just grant it", one European banker told me back in 2006.

In 2007, the financial sector total assets weight was equiva-lent to 89% of the US's GDP; whereas in Europe this figure was 320%, according to the ECB. In 2010, private capital accounted for over 25% of the United States' funding; in Europe, it was less than 4%. Some accused the Anglo-Saxon countries of attacking Europe out of envy; others blamed Germany, which by 2011 had deposited 23% of its GDP in aid for periphery countries. In truth, since 2001, Europe has been through the most aggressive de-industrialisation process ever seen in the OECD area, with a decline of gross value added (GVA) of 24%, according to EU figures. The GVA of Spanish industry in 2012 accounted for 15.1% of the total, barely half what it was 35 years previously.

This decline didn't come about by chance. It was the result of interventionist policies, heavy taxation, legal uncertainty and disproportionate energy costs. There was the unilateral introduction of a tax on carbon dioxide emissions, the imposition of arbitrary taxes on any industry (telecommunications, engineering and electricity) that generated reasonable profit margins, trade union control of all aspects of labour activity, threats to expropriate companies like ArcelorMittal or Total for attempting to downsize the workforce in sectors with overcapacity and inefficiency problems (steel and refining). All this in addition to retroactive changes to legislation and regulation in a number of countries, Spain included, culminating in public administrations not paying their bills and pushing sectors such as environmental services, cleaning and water management to the edge.

This de-industrialisation had a problem. It could not be easily reversed, and the trillions of debt spent on building infrastructures and capacity to accommodate "future growth" were still there, awaiting the arrival of the unicorns. Meanwhile, the costs were being passed on to the ordinary taxpayer, which meant less consumption and a sharp decline in domestic demand.

The explosion of the debt crisis highlighted the failures of European integration and of the single currency, and of the difficulty the peripheral countries had when surmounting their mounting level of debt and expenditure. All this led to fears of a break-up of the euro, owing to the impossibility of bailing out all the problematic states.

By 2014, we started to see signs of optimism in Europe supported by a macroeconomic environment that, while far from attractive, was showing some encouraging data. But the fragility of the recovery was still high.

- Industrial production indices are approaching expansive levels.
- Corporate margins are improving, quietly, thanks to exports and cost control.
- Private debt has been reduced to 2006 levels.

- Financing costs for small and medium-sized enterprises (SMEs), including in Spain and Italy, fell to a two-year low. Gas imports increased for the first time since 2008, which was very relevant to industrial activity.

All these elements themselves should not lead us to be overly optimistic, but neither should they be ignored.

Recovery continues to be extremely weak since, at the same time, countries persist in tax rises and attacks on disposable income that depress consumption. And if we don't see an improvement of consumption, all other variables are simply smoke.

Unemployment and consumption are the two great scourges of Europe. With all the government support and a highly interventionist state, the unemployment figure in France has reached three million; in Spain, above 5.8 million, a moderate slowdown in job losses. But job creation is only going to happen when consumption recovers, and that will not happen in an environment where disposable income is curtailed and taxes destroy families and SMEs. The fiscal burden in the EU is already about 40%.

Threatening to raise taxes on big business now is another huge mistake. They've been a pillar of internationalisation and growth, and thanks to them we now have global multinationals, employing tens of thousands. But these strategic moves represent a significant risk and cost for shareholders thanks to rising debt and weakening balance sheets. The cleaning of such balance sheets has not been completed in full, despite cost savings and divestitures, and to raise taxes is a dangerous move that does more harm than good because these large corporations are also big employers, generate the bulk of private investment in the countries and their social security contributions are one of the main guarantees of the financial sustainability of the welfare systems. Further tax changes would also delay the entry of foreign capital until conditions were stable and attractive.

The EU has warned France that it cannot go higher in its tax burden. Unfortunately, as always, tax hikes will delay the recovery and won't generate the desired revenues.

Tax increases do not help consumption or employment, and nor do they improve the economies of those countries that are in debt. Keep in mind that at the end of 2013 the debt to GDP in the euro area may exceed the current 90.6% by at least 1%, and that the state deficits continue to rise above 4%. In this environment of low interest rates and moderate-risk premiums, there seems to be little problem, but low interest rates and strong bond demand will not last forever.

But the relative calm in Europe cannot mask the huge debt problem across the eurozone as European countries, and peripherals in particular, are going to have to face excessive deficit budgets.

So why be optimistic?

The financial impact of the crisis can be lessened by using short-term financing. Not only that, Germany and the other paying countries will continue to press for much-needed structural reform. And so it is likely that these aggressive measures (similar to the ones taken by Japan and the US to help the financial system) will backfire owing to the risk of higher interest rates and possible bumps in the huge portfolio of government debt that banks accumulate, instead of eventually successfully dealing with the problem. European banks accumulate up to 20% of Europe's sovereign debt and that weight is monitored constantly by the ECB.

But, like other liquidity injections, the problem will remain if a slight recovery is seen as an opportunity to increase the tax pressure and delay the reform of governments that spend between €10 and €50 billion more than they collect structurally. Because then we will find the same problem as in previous periods of slight improvements: the bureaucratic machine crushes the recovery.

CHAPTER TWELVE

WHY WAS THE BREAK-UP OF THE EURO FEARED?

Between 2011 and 2012, the break-up of the euro was one of the great debates in the City. I was never convinced it would happen, but the fear was there, and it was echoed in newspapers, on the radio and TV and in conversations with friends.

Now it all seems a bad dream and there could be a quantitative easing programme in Europe as growth resumes.

And no one talks of the break-up of the euro any more. Thanks to the magic words of Mario Draghi, president of the ECB: "Within our mandate, the ECB is ready to do whatever it takes to preserve the euro. And believe me, it will be enough." Since then, peripheral credit default swaps have collapsed to 2009 levels and bond yields are back to pre-crisis levels. This without spending a single euro on stimulus.

Those who feared the break-up of the euro put forward three fundamental reasons for their anxiety:

- The need to refinance European countries (€1.3 trillion in 2013), coupled with the inevitable contraction of their GDPs, could lead them to incur expenses exceeding 30% of their total revenues. And the solution advocated by some to increase expenditure in order to support GDP is easily challenged with examples from the past, such as the unnecessary spending on infrastructure discussed above.

- A couple of countries cannot bail out everyone else. To claim that this is a problem of the peripheral countries is incorrect. The problem of debt included France and central European countries. France's debt ratio would exceed 115% of its GDP in 2014 and it has yet to find a way to bail out its leading banks, whose assets account for 240% of the country's GDP.[14]
- The only positive effect of remaining in the euro is to be able to receive funding at attractive rates and hold a strong currency in a protective trade and financial environment. If these benefits are lost, the social and political cost of staying in the euro (compared to the possibility of withdrawing and being able to devalue local currency and refinance debt) is too high. In other terms, the financial cost of maintaining the single currency doesn't compensate for the economic and social burden that the citizens would have to shoulder.

What made it difficult for the euro to break up?

The problem this would cause to the banking system, and the sheer weight that the system has within the European economy – 320% of Europe's GDP – is exactly what made a break-up difficult. The other reason is that Germany would go into a deep recession, its currency would appreciate dramatically and it would lose exports, since it sells 65% of its goods and services to the EU.

Harmonised fiscal union is the only solution to save the euro. The options to reject this are ever more limited, but is it acceptable? How long would it take to implement? Can we believe in a European Union that has never known how to cut

---

[14] http://www.oecd-ilibrary.org/economics/government-debt_gov-debt-table-en

its budget? Who would guarantee its execution? Who would impose fines and penalties, and how? Would they be paid up? Fiscal restraint already forms part of EU regulation, yet it has been bypassed by absolutely everyone. And the key question: do we truly believe that Europe will attract capital if the tax burden mounts while GDP contracts?

Printing money would not work, because the euro is used in less than 20% of transactions worldwide. Those who call for Europe to print money think it's a great idea. It would lower the debt in devalued euros, create a little inflation and incentivise competition, wouldn't it? No. It would generate excessive inflation because those euros are not used globally. It doesn't work in the United States, despite the fact that 75% of all global transactions are done in dollars, or in the United Kingdom, with the City as its driving force. The perennial devaluation model doesn't work; it only generates a massive transfer of money from efficient countries to debtor countries.

From the return of confidence in the eurozone to the possibility of a quantitative easing programme, many things had changed. But structural issues remained. "Of course any private or public assets that we might buy would have to meet certain quality standards," said Jens Weidmann, a member of the ECB's Governing Council, in an interview with MNI.

However, the European ABS market is too small (€300bn–€450bn) for a €1 trillion QE and the challenges would be high when buying sovereign debt in order to adhere to the ECB mandate.

There are three options for the ECB: yield curves, regional differences and credit spreads, which would be targeted in the ECB's version of unconventional monetary policies. According to HSBC, some of the measures are more akin to credit easing (CE) than quantitative easing (QE). It is also apparent that the approach is more qualitative because if the ECB is to make purchases it will take into account valuations.

The ECB would choose from different options, which reflects the bank-based intermediation that dominates in the eurozone, unlike in the US, where the main focus of QE has been Treasuries and mortgage-backed securities. As a possibility, the ECB could choose a normalisation of haircuts on its collateral.

There is also the issue of the "no deflation yet" debate. The ECB needs more time to see whether there really is a price deflation issue. So far, data suggests otherwise. No deflation, just disinflation due to overcapacity and previous bubbles.

When you have invested (spent) hundreds of billions of euros on "industrial plans" and productive capacity, especially in energy, car industry, textile, retail and infrastructure, you will experience a reduction of prices because of the competition between oversized sectors, an overcapacity of up to 40% in some cases. On the other hand, inflation exists in other elements, which is very relevant to industry and consumption, such as energy costs.

The "alleged risk of deflation" is the excuse of governments to justify greater financial repression, trying to create false inflation through rate cuts while citizens have less purchasing power or through monetary stimulus plans when tax rises lead nowhere.

To reactivate the economy governments should return money to the pockets of citizens who have stoically accepted and paid for interventionist policies and supported schemes and incentives that have led the EU to spend up to 3% of its GDP to destroy 4.5 million jobs and sink the economy.

> *The balance sheet of central banks is like the opening scene in* Wall-E.
>
> Trader's comment

However, most analysts and strategists are betting on the continuation of the head-in-the-sand policy, which I call "pretend and extend". Liquidity is injected into the system while the ECB lowers interest rates and buys bonds. In short, an increase in debt: as *Wall-E* does with the rubbish in the Pixar film, debt is hidden and packaged rather than repaid. And the problem would concern not just Italy or Spain but also France.

The solution to the European debt crisis is clear. No more rising public spending, no more debt and no imposition of QE. After spending trillions of dollars on expansionist policies without any conclusive, positive results, we should begin to grasp that this cure does more harm than good. All these mechanisms have proved to be ineffective.

We have had five consecutive years of stimulus in Europe. Providing liquidity must be a temporary measure, not a structural one. Half a trillion a year is madness. In the meantime, the obvious solution lies in exercising fiscal prudence, putting a stop to spiralling spending for political ends, cleaning up the banks' balance sheets – preferably done by shareholders and bondholders – and attracting capital.

CHAPTER THIRTEEN

EVIL SPECULATORS: SOMEONE ELSE IS TO BLAME

Once the debt crisis was evident worldwide, the excuses began again.

The investor's legitimate decision "not to buy" was called an "attack". An attack on our inalienable right to gain access to the investor's pocket whenever we want, however we want and what's more – of course – at a low cost, in order to spend it as we please with no inconvenient questions asked or accountability for the use of the money. A right that we obviously denied any emerging country, even the Hispanic ones, as in their case it seemed perfectly logical that the risk premium would increase by the day. In the countries where our companies were investing, country risk was a "fair valuation measure". In our case, it was an "attack". And naturally, we demanded that investors buy our bonds, albeit unwillingly.

The sovereign debt crisis bore many similarities to the "property bubble". An "overvalued asset" (in this case, state debt, unjustifiably regarded as a risk-free asset), a drastic rise in inventory (all countries issuing debt, resorting to domestic banks, pension funds and social security to place it) and bust (when the borrowing capacity maximises).

Indeed, the property bubble could not have expanded without the state credit bubble, without exorbitant lending by the savings banks – all public – and without the monstrous and unjustified sums "invested in" – spent on – pointless infrastructure, which saw Spain build ghost cities, ghost airports and an unused high-speed train for a network comparable only to China.

The outcome will be the same as the subprime mortgage crisis: a devaluation of underlying asset (sovereign debt) in keeping with real demand.

The reaction was typical: first, disbelief ("but we have the soundest financial system in the world"), then anger ("Spain is not Greece"), followed by a state of denial ("the risk premium is rising owing to external attacks") and, lastly, acknowledgement. And this is where, finally, the solution begins. Sovereign debt will become more expensive, states will learn not to squander capital and the debt-based growth model – namely the funding of privileges acquired by a declining society with supposed revenue from future generations – will come to an end.

We also forget that the oasis of free debt is a recent invention. Less than twenty years ago, European states paid up to double the current interest rates with economies that grew annually. They didn't have a debt ratio of 120% of their GDP, and unemployment was at an acceptable level. The exponential access to credit following the entry into Europe also triggered the policy of "spend as fast as possible and as much as we can". We may blame the markets or whomever we wish, but the comments making the rounds on speculators lead me to ask the following questions:

- What could be more speculative than a government that presents GDP and deficit predictions it knows it will not meet?
- Who can expect commitments to long-term investments when all political decisions are made with a view to the short term?

- How can we resolve snowballing debt in Europe when social agents are demanding more spending and thus more debt?

Investors, who are customers, have as much right to try to protect themselves when they perceive a high risk as consumers have when they purchase a home or a car. Investors seek to protect themselves in the face of excess and bad practice on the sell-side, and above all from those who rule the roost: governments. This is where the credit default swaps (CDSs) make their entrance.

Credit default swaps

A credit default swap is an instrument that protects the bond investor from the possibility that the issuer (be it a state or a corporation) defaults on a payment. As the idea spread that "state debt is a risk-free asset", CDSs became extremely valuable as it was discovered that states are not only a risk but a big one. However, as with other types of insurance, a CDS loses its capability to mitigate risk in the event of a disaster on a monumental scale, since it simply would not be able to pay up. When the probability of default is above 70%, the coverage has almost zero value. If a country defaults, its swap is rarely collected.

Countries and their institutions believed that a CDS market of some $24 trillion was an ample sum to cover the credit risk. Why? Because only corporate bonds were believed to entail risk, whereas sovereign debt would not need huge default insurance contracts – until countries began to engage in madly issuing debt, creating a huge bond bubble that is currently almost impossible to insure. Who assumes the risk of guaranteeing this debt when banks and state lending institutions are still struggling to crawl out of their own particular debt holes? To those who blame it on evil private capitalists, we should not omit to mention that over half the Spanish financial system was public: the savings banks. And we cannot forget that all the main Spanish political parties and the two trade unions were represented on the boards of those banks, all of whom eagerly signed the accounts of these entities.

Eighty-nine per cent of these CDSs are in the same hands as those which hold the sovereign debt: the domestic and central banks.[15] The principal CDS positions are in Italy, Germany, Spain, Brazil and Greece, although the figures by no means compare with those in the United States, or, much more tellingly, those belonging to General Electric, Bank of America, JPMorgan and Goldman Sachs: combined, these exceed Italy and Spain together (figures from November 2012).

---

[15] Source HSBC: "Credit Default Swap Market Analysis", December 2012.

CHAPTER FOURTEEN

SNOWBALLING DEBT

We owe billions. Who does everybody in the world owe money to? And why don't we just kill the bastards and relax?

Tommy Tiernan, Irish comedian

Let's examine the factors that produce the snowball effect, despite the appeals for calm.

The agencies took years to show in their ratings what the market already presumed, namely the economic fragility of the debtor countries. When the credit downgrades finally came, no one in any government expected them. The successive rescue packages to Greece, Portugal and Ireland left the financial systems almost without the means to address similar exposures in other countries.

Optimistic dreams of growth forecasts and debt reduction. Without a rise in GDP, unemployment doesn't fall and debt increases. And more importantly, without policies for business growth, state revenue will consume the interest payments and expenditure that generates no return (GDP), which some call "social", and which are no more than loans that will come out of the future earnings of our children.

Governments don't like it to be known that there is no demand for their product; therefore they look for associates and friends to fill the shop so it doesn't look empty. And then (when they are issuing debt and demanding money from the evil speculators destined only to cover the interest and not the principal), they ask for the credit tap to be opened further. In spite of the cuts already announced, there is a need for a deeper reduction in expenditure to cover the cash deficit and the interest, and few take note of this. "The fault lies with those evil investors" who have the gall to expect to recover their investment and demand an appropriate price for the risk assumed. Really...

The market, which attracts such hatred from interventionists, reacts because it has been lied to. And it reacts by selling and seeking protection, or by choosing not to buy.

Debt is a drug. And like all drug addicts, we always feel we have the situation under control. "My debt to GDP ratio is lower than Japan's", "it won't happen to me", "Spain is not Greece" or the equivalent "my colleague is worse off" currently in vogue: "private debt is greater".

The credit risk is felt in the terrible effect known as "crowding out", when the state monopolises the available credit and drives down credit access to families and private enterprise. Public authorities saw their credit access increase during the economic crisis, whereas small and medium-sized enterprises (SMEs) sectors lost dramatically, according to the ECB.

The banks were rescued worldwide in order to stop the public administration credit bubble from bursting. And this would not be a problem if it created wealth rather than covered current expenditure, but when states "invest" they do so on pointless infrastructures and the cost of that debt is repaid with tax revenue and less credit.

Debt in itself is not bad. Debt is bad when it generates no return. And, as in any economic activity, there are acceptable "social investments" that don't generate economic returns, but these cannot exceed investments that yield returns, because otherwise we fall into a spending spiral that leads to more debt and more taxation, more impoverishment, lower earnings, the same expenditure, more debt and bankruptcy.

Let's be clear. There will be no real recovery without confidence in the state and in the financial sector. Therefore, austerity and healthy public accounts are foremost for everything. Credit, private growth and social rights.

Towards the end of 2013, many people were telling me that "the banks are making a killing by borrowing from the ECB at 1% and buying public debt at 5%". There were several errors in this belief.

From the point of view of the investor, the bank was running a very high risk. Rather than a "gravy train", it was the state's implicit imposition that compelled the domestic banks to purchase its bonds for the purpose of making that famous headline: "the Treasury successfully issues..." Of course it had: the banks had bought them!

However, the risk of such an investment, despite the high yield, falls on the principal and on the weight of exposure to sovereign debt. It's like saying you earn a lot because you buy a home and then lease it to an investor. And then you buy all the houses in the area and rent them to the same investor. Suddenly, the investor stops paying the rent, or the properties lose value on account of the accumulation of risk, or a commune of crooks sets up camp in your back garden. Your "attractive" investment becomes ruinous. When the state controls both credit and bank investment, the risk and the level of dependency are immense.

The need to balance the books, stop wasteful spending and moderate debt has a direct relationship with social rights. How?

The public institutions, social security, pensions and other services have huge resources (more than 90% in some cases)
invested in public debt. Some argue that it's a good idea to
concentrate most of the resources of these bodies in a single
financial instrument – sovereign debt. Prudent risk and portfolio management are ignored. All this has been decided by some
advisory committees that charge for their services and will not
be held accountable if this explodes. In France, social security
invests a maximum of 44% in its sovereign debt, while the
eurozone average is 25%.

If the state continues to borrow and create an unproductive
expenditure deficit from which it cannot escape, its eventual
default will lead these institutions to bankruptcy. That's why I
don't understand why people demand we stop paying off debt.

CHAPTER FIFTEEN

THE DAMNED RISK PREMIUM

In 2014, there is little talk about peripheral bond yields and spreads against Germany. The difference between the cost of borrowing of the peripheral countries and Germany has shrunk in two years from all-time highs back to pre-crisis levels. However, bond yield spreads were making headlines in the press all over Europe in 2010–2011.

This is what I wrote then:

> I often read things like: "The risk premium is rising due to an attack by the market". I long to see a headline one day that reads: "The risk premium is rising because the institutions can no longer absorb any more debt than that which has already been placed on them."

Bill Gross, of the largest fixed-income asset fund, PIMCO, said: "Greece was a zit, Portugal is a boil, Spain is a tumour."

What is the risk premium?

The risk premium is the minimum return required by bond buyers from a specific state, in contrast to the return on a low-risk asset. In the Spanish case, the yield spread is measured against the German bond, considered Europe's lowest risk bond. The risk premium is therefore an indicator of both the investor's appetite to buy and current demand in the secondary debt market. It's the price investors are prepared to pay according to the risk they perceive in the economy of the country.

But there is only investor appetite if it is backed by a low default risk. No matter how many interventionist measures are put in place, investors will not buy bonds if they don't see numbers that are reliable, verifiable and consistent, as well as an improvement in the economy and the ability to repay debt. The risk premium did not rise on account of any attack, nor was the risk of the break-up of the euro a crucial factor. The risk premium ignored the fact that we were spending between 20 and 25% more than we were earning annually. It simply rose because state bondholders, who watched debt mount and the risk of economic stagnation increase, would not run the risk for such a low return, because that would be like making a donation.

Ninety-six per cent of sovereign CDSs are held by the same semi-state "flagship" institutions that are up to their necks in hundreds of billions in sovereign European debt. These institutions seek protection and cannot sell, thus they suffer low liquidity and a lack of buyers. In the next debt auction, however, they will nevertheless be "urged" to purchase once again. In 2012, Spanish banks amassed more than €200 trillion in government bonds. That is no bargain. It's a considerable risk, with the added problem that purchase capacity falls due to saturation and the refinancing needs of indebted states rise.

Three major points should be taken into account regarding the bond market:

- cost, or the risk premium, will continue rising if capital is not repaid
- as the deleveraging of the banks accelerates, the amount of available money to invest in sovereign debt falls
- the predatory effect of the state on the possibility of funding the private sector undermines the prospects of recovery.

The risk premium becomes a problem when it surpasses 300 basis points, because this shows that the liquidity injections are not working. They bail out those who got it wrong and give others an incentive to do the same – by reaching into the saver's pocket to give money to the indebted squanderer. Worse still, the placebo effect lasts less and less. The inability of even the placement entities to absorb the state debt auctions is a huge problem. As there is almost no domestic demand for debt, it is absorbed among banks and citizens, through the social security or other institutions that have invested up to 90% of their cash in sovereign debt. What's going on?

If the budgets are austere and everything is being undertaken as it should, why is there a lack of investor confidence and talk of the need for a bailout? Do investors want Europe to go bust? I know of no one in the market who wishes Spain or Portugal to go under. Under any circumstances. Because Spain, indeed, is not Greece. Its economy is several times bigger than Greece's, and as such it cannot be simply "bailed out". If Spain collapses, the impact on the S&P 500 and Euro Stoxx, as on Germany and the rest of the EU, would be enormous.

So, if there's no wish to see Europe fall, budgets are moderate and the deficit is being cut... what's going on?

Neither one thing nor the other. The budgets don't convince the sovereign-debt fixed-income investor, neither in terms of revenue nor in terms of expenditure. While they appear very optimistic, they don't seem to lessen the role of the state in the economy and barely reduce the deficit. Meanwhile, the debt:GDP

122 Life in the Financial Markets

ratio increases. It's true that cuts are being imposed to pay interest, but the bloated public administration structure between the state and the autonomous regions is the same as ever. Only a radical change here would improve our credit quality.

How is it possible that no one in the different governments is able to understand that the state structure needs to be improved if investors are to regain confidence and start investing again? To my mind, there are three underlying reasons:

- Governments around the globe believe that investor capital must flow to them no matter what. They assume that access to credit is eternal and infinite.
- When governments try to "interact" or "receive feedback" from the market, they often do so through corporate bankers, who, by definition, tend to give them a bright, sugar-covered outlook of the world. Sellers are mistaken to trust analysis from an intermediary. Few governments speak to end-investors.
- Governments, like companies, think they will "calm" the investor by hiding invoices, delaying debt repayments, undermining data and reallocating expenses. They believe that "the less information, the better", which is a total mistake. However, it's a widespread communication practice among companies and governments.

A fixed-income bond investor will not accept 5 or 6% interest rates on ten-year bonds from a state that together with its autonomous regions will most likely gobble up 125% of its revenues in the same period. When revising the growth rates on the downfall, the investor asks himself: "Where will the money come from?"

If the bond buyer doesn't see with crystalline clarity that the risk of losing his capital is minimal, he doesn't buy. He prefers to buy American or German or Swiss bonds at almost negative real interest rates than these "set-piece gravy trains" at higher rates that we are offering him. It's not an image problem or due to having read a downbeat report by an evil speculator – in fact, most reports are upbeat – but because the solvency indicators are poor. If the evil speculator blunders and everything goes well, great. In a month, all sorted: the macroeconomic results will be published and we'll surprise everyone.

The total assets held in all the world's hedge funds (including sectorial, macro, fixed-income, variable, emerging markets and commodities) amount to over $2 trillion. Were everyone to reach an agreement, even those who don't invest in bonds (and everybody will agree with me that this is ridiculous), they would say that they wouldn't have anywhere near the impact that the ECB did before raising its debt, with $4 trillion being flooded into the markets. If the speculator is wrong, he will lose his money and that's the end of it. But what if he doesn't get it wrong and simply makes an adequate analysis and invests his money to prove it?

Be careful not to sneer at the investors' opinion, or think that Bill Gross or Peter Schiff (or – with the utmost modesty – me) simply go against Spain while the politicians, who have never met their commitments, are the real defenders. Who can one trust most? Those who are risking their money and hence analysing reality or those that charge – or win votes – for disguising it?

Let's be clear about one thing. No one, and definitely no investor, expects the country to rescind from spending on basic services like education, health or research. The investor only expects the government to adjust expenditure to revenue. Those who decide to curb expenses but maintain official cars, television stations for the autonomous regions, zombie companies, public administrations multiplied by 17, embassies, grants and subsidies are the politicians elected to manage these resources. The investor only expects to see that resources be managed on the basis of reasonable tax revenue and according to the demand for bonds that the country can assume. Spain cannot be, even if it wanted, more than 30% of the European supply of fixed-income bonds.

The trend is clear. Sovereign risk is being re-evaluated. That debt which for decades we were told was risk-free. Just as we were told that "house prices never fall".

Words and good intentions are worthless. Credibility is not earned by an act of faith. It's earned through action. Until Spain publishes better figures of its credit quality that are clear, unmistakable and sustainable, it's difficult to see the risk premium dropping to the more reasonable levels of 50 basis points. Bond investors do not distinguish between political parties or governments. It's a question of state compliance. And if the state doesn't comply, the investor won't grant his capital.

Would you do so? Would you invest in a business where the manager didn't fulfil his or her targets or massaged outcomes?

Today, no one seems to worry about these matters any more, but credit cycles happen. When excess liquidity dries up, countries that have not done their homework will see the risk premium overshoot again.

CHAPTER SIXTEEN

DERIVATIVES: WEAPONS OF MASS DESTRUCTION?

A constant in the press or in politics in recent years (and especially since 2008) is that derivatives are always mentioned with negative connotations. All opinions should be respected, but not when they are based on objectively erroneous information, and rarely is an attack on derivatives not accompanied by an objectively erroneous comment.

My good friend Eduardo Montero Larraz, a former colleague in London, helps us to shed some light on this subject.

What is a derivative? A derivative is just a financial instrument that derives its value from another financial instrument – from a telecom share or the price of a barrel of petroleum. The range of financial instruments that encompasses this term makes it the only correct definition.

The most famous investor (and one of the most successful) of the last 50 years, Warren Buffett, qualifies derivatives as weapons of mass destruction. This doesn't prevent him from actively using these instruments to manage the risks on his investments. In the following sections, we will examine some examples of their use.

How long have derivatives been around?

A common misunderstanding is that derivatives are very new instruments. People have been using derivatives since the existence of agriculture and trade. The Old Testament refers to financial contracts between farmers in Galilee that are identical to the futures which are quoted every day on the Chicago Stock Exchange. In the Roman Empire, derivatives were used on crops and metals. There are examples of the use of derivatives in all periods of history, so they are not new, and nor is their use confined to investment fund managers with expert knowledge of mathematics and malicious intentions.

What are they used for?

As we mentioned above, the term covers a wide range of financial instruments, but their common denominator is that they are used to manage risk, either to lower it or to increase it.

We all manage risk in our daily dealings; when someone takes out an insurance policy on a home, they are lowering their risk of being unable to deal with unforeseen situations, such as a leak or a short circuit, in exchange for cost in the form of a premium for the insurance company. A greengrocer increases his risk when he orders fifty kilos of apples to improve his sales margin. His risk is that if he doesn't sell them they will rot on his shelves.

Futures are without a doubt the oldest and simplest derivatives. They will exist in any society where trade is carried out. They are the first derivative products referred to in the Old Testament. A future, as its name suggests, is an agreement to exchange a good at an established price on a specific date. A farmer, for example, enters into an agreement with a bread maker to sell him three tonnes of wheat for $800,000, nine months after making the deal. The famer benefits from this contract by securing a price for his crop regardless of the price of wheat at the time of the agreement, and the bread maker likewise secures a price at which he can purchase the commodity for its production. Both agents lessen their uncertainty.

At nine months, irrespective of the price of wheat at that moment, the producer will deliver three tonnes of wheat to the factory at a price of $800,000. It is possible that nine months after the agreement the price of three tonnes of wheat will be exactly $800,000, but in all likelihood the price will have changed, say to $750,000. In this case, if the future contract had not been set, the producer could have purchased the cheapest product and the farmer would have had to sell the wheat at a lower price than the one he secured; the opposite might also have happened if at nine months the price had been $850,000.

Does this mean – unless the settled price coincides with the real price on the day of delivery – that one of the parties will always win and the other always lose? Not necessarily. Both seller and buyer know that the price will fluctuate during this period, and it's possible that when they agreed to the transaction they were both of the opinion that the development of the price could be unfavourable, meaning it was in their interest to fix it beforehand. Yet it's also possible that regardless of their view on which way the price of wheat would go they would seek to lessen their risk and know for certain at what price they could close the deal in order to facilitate their production decisions.

In short, the logic of the transaction may be speculative or may be simple risk reduction. In the latter case, the transaction may prove beneficial to both parties.

Purpose and uses of derivatives

As discussed above, the purpose of any derivative is to manage risk in order to lower or increase it. A wheat producer who sells his crop in advance reduces his risk. A wheat speculator who buys the crop from this producer without being able to make use of the wheat increases his risk, as he believes the price of wheat will be higher after nine months.

We have already explained who uses derivatives, which put simply can be grouped into end-users and speculators. In the example of the wheat, the end-users are the producers and the industrial users of wheat, whose business is subject to the price fluctuations of this commodity. The speculators are the agents who have a vision of which way the price of wheat will go and carry out transactions to make a profit if their assumptions are confirmed.

Thus, it's easy to classify group 1 as legitimate users and group 2 as parasites of the system, yet the differences are not so obvious if we consider the case in more depth. In the first place, group 1 in its purest form doesn't exist, since all producers and industrial users incorporate a speculative element into their decisions. The wheat producer only plants the crop if he thinks that the price at which he can sell will exceed his costs. Otherwise, he would not produce wheat (at least that year), so his business may also be labelled "speculative". On the other hand, the end-users of commodities like wheat don't only operate in the market based on production or consumption estimates. They often choose not to cover production according to a positive vision of prices, or to cover a larger amount of what they expect to produce or consume if they have a negative view of future price developments, which are all purely speculative activities.

Let's look at the role of a pure market speculator rather than the partial one we have described above. This speculator will purchase wheat as a future, or option, when he believes the price is going to rise, and will sell the wheat when he thinks it will fall. Who will buy futures from or sell them to the speculator? There are only two options: another speculator or an industrial user. If the transaction entered into is between two pure speculators, the net effect of the speculation in the market is neutral. One buys and the other sells the same product for the same settlement date. By contrast, if the transaction between a speculator and an industrial user is agreed upon, the speculator facilitates a transaction that the industrial user might not have been able to carry out without the presence of the speculator. Therefore, the speculator is contributing liquidity to the market.

Another role played by the speculator is to offer flexibility to industrial users. If a producer wishes to sell a crop in nine months' time, but the user wants to buy in eight months and they are unable to reach a compromise, a speculator can buy the production at nine months and sell it at eight in the same moment, with a view to unwind the commitment with a profit in five months with other producers. In this case, the presence of the speculator has facilitated the transaction between the two end-users.

Speculators assume the risk in the market, which at times generates a return and at others incurs a loss. The speculator cannot enter into an agreement if he doesn't find another party who is interested in the contrary, be they a speculator or end-user.

Thanks to Eduardo Montero Larraz, head of structured products in Europe, CIBC.

CHAPTER SEVENTEEN

THE ILLUSION OF EASY MONEY: THE INVESTMENT BANKS AND THE GREAT DECEPTION

The great error of the debt crisis, incorrectly called the financial crisis, was that everyone – operators, governments, families, analysts and investors – had got used to the idea that debt wasn't a problem.

Debt is a drug, as I have mentioned throughout this book. It numbs normally prudent valuation criteria and makes us feel strong and powerful. It makes us see everything, even the future, through rose-tinted glasses. But this is an illusion because debt, like drug addiction, is nothing less than an enslavement which starts from the time it's no longer possible to pay it back. We don't know how to function without it. We don't know why we have lost our strength. We ask ourselves, "Why is this happening to me?" What's more, the worst side to debt is that it impoverishes everyone. We hear about those who have benefited from the crisis, but any numerical analysis will prove that the bursting of the bubble has only resulted in losses, risk and more debt for the majority of market operators and their clients.

Everyone was convinced they could accumulate and handle debt better than anyone else, and thought they were immune.

And so, central banks and governments kept interest rates down, pumping money into the economy and printing more of it. Everything was fine, because the "fairy godmother" of the Federal Reserve, the Bank of Japan, the European Central Bank or the Bank of England would always be there to come to our aid.

When central banks and governments push everyone to take more risks, this sends a message that all is well and that they will provide a safety net to anyone who falls over the cliff. The problem was that all the operators threw themselves over the edge, and the net could not hold that much weight. The domino effect that states create when they compel operators to take more and more risk is never properly evaluated. In each case, the same problem of bubbles and collapse arises.

Lehman Brothers, Bear Stearns, the subprime crisis. The one overall error that has been proved is the presumption that the banks had infinite leverage. That investment banks, with a great team of professionals behind them, could afford high levels of debt because they were making substantial and predictable profits. Until the saturation of debt accumulation and risk concentration – two bombs that explode at the same time, producing a domino effect on all types of assets, be they quality or toxic ones.

But we want to resolve this crisis of irresponsible lending by borrowing more. We all demand our right to borrow more and more in this terribly selfish downturn in which we are all spending our grandchildren's money.

And we need someone to blame.

If I am lent money, the bank is bad. No matter that I have asked for it of my own free will. We place the blame on the lender. The borrower is a poor victim who has been tricked. "Germany profited from our property bubble", "The bank granted me a mortgage that I couldn't pay" and so forth. This is not a situation of lender–borrower co-responsibility. It has never been so. The greatest responsibility falls on the party who takes out the credit. At least this is how it was until the present. Now it's the borrower countries who *demand* credit conditions from those who lend to them.

To play the victim and claim that "they made a mistake by giving us a loan" is bad business. If we fail in our commitment as payers, if we hide behind excuses (like "the person who gave me the loan is to blame") without also accepting that we are partly responsible for believing we were able to absorb debt eternally, we simply lose our credibility as credit operators. Then, no one will give us credit. However, we often not only read that "we must not pay our debt" but that, moreover, "Germany/the ECB/the EU should allow us a higher deficit ceiling and more debt." In short, we should not only be commitment-free borrowers but also with-strings-attached borrowers.

As a Finnish MEP said, "if I lend a friend €1,000 and they spend it on partying, that doesn't mean I must continue lending money to them, and more cheaply; nor will I write off the €1,000 they still owe me."

We didn't create this spiral as a result of evil. For decades, our collective subconscious has been hearing from countries and governments about unpaid debt. I remember when my parents finished paying off the mortgage on their house. They went out to celebrate. Today, this would seem crazy. Why not renegotiate the mortgage and extend it? Then we could buy another car.

We have also discussed our need to lay the blame on someone other than ourselves. It gives us peace, justifies us and, not least, gives us a scapegoat as an excuse for our next error. This type of distant and vague guilty party is the typical sort to crop up in our macroeconomic discussions with relatives and friends.

One of the most hilarious scapegoats of 2012 emerged in a letter published in the *New York Times*, which later became a book, *Why I Left Goldman Sachs*. A senior executive resigns and recognises the skulduggery of Goldman Sachs! We were right! The dictatorship of the markets unveiled by an employee.

As a customer of Goldman Sachs, I personally have never felt manipulated, cheated or treated like a puppet. I have also worked in an investment bank, and the supposed revelations of the occult practices of Goldman Sachs expose nothing more than the aggressive environment that is the financial market, and a sub-universe of derivatives, seen through the eyes of an angry middle manager.

An investment bank is not a father or a grandmother. It's an organisation that seeks to maximise returns, like myself, and it offers a range of services that I, as a trained professional, must analyse, buy and evaluate in terms of risk. Among the many media uproars, it seems that we forget that we are all adults here. The reason we are being paid is to make calibrated decisions in order to not be blindly led by a consultancy, be it Goldman Sachs, McKinsey or any other.

Worker talking nonsense about his clients? First, if there is one bank where one can anonymously report such practices, it is Goldman. Notwithstanding, everyone else says things they shouldn't about others. Any manager recognises that the buy recommendations of large banks are known as "the kiss of death", because they usually perform disastrously on the second day of publication. The business of the financial markets is not that of an NGO, nor is it conducted in a politically correct environment. It's an environment where everyone is under pressure to produce results. If they don't like it, they should send their CV to a ministry, where they can spend an unlimited budget very correctly.

Goldman Sachs is not a state-owned organisation, nor is it public-orientated. It received money from TARP and returned it with interest. How I would love to see Spanish savings banks return even a penny. It's not a commercial bank either, and has never offered retail services. It has no business other than acting as an intermediary between qualified professionals, who are fully aware of the risks they are taking. Goldman Sachs doesn't sell preference shares to grannies who know nothing of this type of instrument, nor does it offer mortgages of 120% of the sales price. Its business model is that of neither Citibank, nor JPMorgan, nor the other banks. And its customers' models aren't either. And I fear there is much playing the victim among those customers who never alerted others to past successes, or even acknowledged them, and now blame the bank for their disasters. Anyone who has signed a procurement of services with an investment bank knows that it sets out every possible risk, including conflicts of interest.

Goldman Sachs is essentially a vast trading house. And the question that we can pose is whether its structure is right for its corporate purpose. Some think that the change of model, from being a partnership-run private bank to a listed entity focused on quarterly results has been harmful.[16] I disagree. The problem is not the quarterly results but the business behind them. And probably this is where the critics are right when they say that the trading revenues have too much weight with regard to the revenue from other divisions, generating a constant need to "create" products and offers.

For many years, the problem of the investment bank model has been that it is simply not profitable. This has led to its transformation from a "banking" model (and one of consultancy) to a "trading" model or, worse, one of corporate public relations. Traders, as I myself have been, do this: buy and sell in exchange for a short-term expected profit. And you already know the public relations model well: "Yes, sir; of course, sir".

Investment banks must regain their independence, return to being leaders, revive the value of fundamental analysis and the business of creating new financing opportunities, stop being so diplomatic and take two steps forward. They should

---

[16] http://www.forbes.com/sites/aroy/2012/03/14/want-to
-improvegoldman-sachs-convert-it-back-into-a-partnership/

leave aside the "commissions" objective in order to return to the goal of "creating business together", in a context in which the bank's interests are aligned with those of its customers.

But the truth is that Goldman Sachs has a reputation for running the world, even though neither its market quota nor its results justify this, simply because many world leaders have worked there. However, no one claims that Harvard, Oxford, Cambridge or Stanford, the universities where the world elite are educated, rule the world. That doesn't sell.

CHAPTER EIGHTEEN

STIMULUS POLICIES AND KICKING THE CAN DOWN THE ROAD

Doctor, I'm an alcoholic, what can you prescribe me?

Three vodkas and a whisky.

Thanks, Dr Bernanke.

Traders' joke

Families have to repay their debt. Governments don't.

Paul Krugman

Many people ask me how an investment fund manager who theoretically benefits from expansionary policies of public spending, monetary stimuli and low interest rates can defend budgetary prudence and criticise interventionism. Simple: because I have three children and I don't want to see them shoulder our debt. What's more, I don't aim to earn a fortune in one year, exploit the latest bubble and then retire.

Fortunately, I'm a workaholic and I want to work for many years, so I'm worried about the short-sightedness of our governments, the placebo effect of pumping money created from thin air into the market and the irrational increase in debt. My grandfather used to say, "You can't get something out of nothing", and spiralling debt and printing money just dig deeper into the hole of the economy.

A few months ago I was playing Monopoly with my son Daniel, who was beating me decisively. I only had 200 dollars left to play with. Dani said to me, "We could make some more banknotes and give them to you." Jaime, another of my sons, exclaimed, "But that's cheating!" and Dani admitted, "That's true. What's the point? And it's unfair, anyway, because I beat you fair and square." A 10-year-old child grasps it perfectly: printing currency is stealing from the saver to give to the debtor. We are selfishly bent on creating inflation and indebting ourselves with a view to passing on the bill to future generations.

In 2006, we had a meeting in Chicago with other investment fund managers. It was a spectacular three-day affair with lots of talks, meetings and debates. And as star guests, besides Colin Powell, US Army General and Secretary of State for Defence, we had the honour of listening to Michael Lewis, author of books such as *Moneyball*, *The Big Short* and *Boomerang*, and, as the highpoint, Alan Greenspan, the former governor of the Federal Reserve.

> *The US can always pay any debt it has because we can always print money to do that.*
>
> Alan Greenspan

The messages reaching us were clear. Debt is not a problem, because interest rates can always be cut and money printed; expenditure isn't a problem either, because it generates GDP; the yields demanded on investments must not be high, because the cost of capital falls... States and central banks were saying "take risks", "ride the wave", "I'll pick you up when you fall".

Alan Greenspan said, "There is a risk. That's why these are extraordinary measures. They cannot be allowed to become a habitual practice." Yet they have become habitual.

For years, I have written much about the macroeconomic environment and new Keynesian policies, and I believe that gradually people are realising that the measures of hiding and expanding, of kicking the can down the road and waiting for everything to clear, not only fix nothing but also exacerbate real economic problems. It's like hiding the dust under the carpet.

> *Paper money eventually returns to its intrinsic value: zero.*
>
> Voltaire

It's easy to forget, but we are going through the most aggressive period of money printing (creation of paper money, fiduciary money) in history. In three years, the amount of monetary stimulus artificially created by central banks across the globe has reached $9 trillion. That's as if every inhabitant on the planet had bought a plasma TV on credit. A staggering amount of debt, with an incalculable impact on growth and employment, as you can see. However, we have become debt junkies and we convince ourselves, as all drug addicts do, that without it, things would have been worse.

In fact, it has been demonstrated that an increase in public expenditure and indebtedness doesn't have a multiplier effect, but rather cannibalises the private sector.

According to figures from the IMF, the United States saw a 7.3% increase in public spending between 2007 and 2011 in order to obtain an 8% fall in real (not nominal) GDP; the United Kingdom's expenditure rose 6.9% in the same period, to obtain an 11% fall in real GDP. And all this debt is savagely devaluing currency and impoverishing the saver. Out of the 34 OECD countries that most stimulate the economy, 90% had the lowest growth in real GDP.

But it's worth reviewing the risks of quantitative easing, or QE, by referring to the magnificent risk analysis drawn up by Credit Suisse and Boenning & Scattergood, among others.

- **Generation of inflation, especially in agricultural and energy commodities.** The markets rise, but company operational results and ordinary earnings continue to fare badly thanks to deterioration in growth. In other words, it doesn't generate corporate wealth or jobs, only inflation in markets and assets.

  Wealth is transferred – indebting the system – from productive activities to financial managers and operators. According to three different studies (D'Amico & King, Yellen and Gagnon), the two previous liquidity injections, called QE1 and QE2, generated an additional annual inflation of between 0.9 and 1.1% of the system.

- **The famous "wealth effect" is not generated.** One of the fallacies of credit expansion is the idea that rising markets and stable house prices create a "perception of wealth", an effect that encourages increased consumption. However, this is not true when disposable income is attacked through rising taxes. People don't rush out to consume when they have lost confidence in the institutional and political system, even less so if they see that inflationary movements don't tally with the productive economy. If all this is accompanied, as until now, by increased job insecurity, so much the worse. And we still have to see the bill for this colossal amount of debt.

- **Economic growth isn't properly supported.** It has been demonstrated that these policies don't improve industrial or manufacturing activity sufficiently or close to the potential, as can be confirmed in the ISM index (an index based on surveys of more than 300 manufacturing firms by the Institute of Supply Management).

Just like drugs, expansionary policies have less effect over time, thus requiring a higher dose. QE3 marked the first time the Federal Reserve did not talk about the sterilisation of assets (meaning instead of selling and buying it would become even more indebted), maintaining the expansion of its balance sheet until "the unemployment situation improved".

The US unemployment rate, however, is, as of 2014, at 6.2%.... or is it? The (U-6) "real" unemployment rate is 12.3% (data from the US Bureau of Labor Statistics).

In April 2014, five years after trillions of dollars' worth of QE, the US Labor Force plunged to 155.421 million while those "Not in the Labor Force" surged to 92.018 million, which is the highest on record. The Workforce Participation Rate fell to 62.81% in April 2014, the lowest since 1978.

Additionally, according to the Bureau of Labor Statistics, 20% of all families in the United States do not have a single member that is employed. Sixty-two per cent of all Americans make $20 or less an hour at this point. The number of Americans receiving benefits from the federal government each month exceeds the number of full-time workers in the private sector by more than 60 million.

The impact on commodities is obvious. On gold and petroleum, because they offer a safe bet in the face of inflation and the fall in the value of currencies in the race to see who prints more and worse; on soft commodities (food), owing to the multiplier effect of exported inflation and the impoverishment of the producer countries thanks to the fall in the value of the dollar.

QE incentivises the junk – or high-yield – bond bubble, because state bonds from low-risk countries sell at an almost negative real return.

The impact on equities is two-fold. On one hand, it fuels more aggressive purchases of the more indebted securities, with worse fundamentals. This is logical, since they are securities in which an improvement in the cost of capital (their discount rate) is more important for the share price than the impairment of their returns, which, don't forget, will continue to go downhill. On the other, it leads the most exposed securities to an inflationary environment with more attractive and expensive multiples.

Stimulus policies create the same risk as massive credit expansion. Furthermore, they don't lower systemic risk: they hide it. Since 2001, the impact of interventionist measures on the intrinsic volatility of assets and the markets has been exponential.

During the crisis, we have seen that, despite interventionist bids by the central banks, the velocity of money circulation continues to slow down. The velocity of the circulation of money measures the frequency at which a unit of currency is transformed into income within a year. It calculates the decline and acceleration of economic activity and wealth creation, which is not recovered despite liquidity injections.

The central banks have created a false money supply equivalent to the amount of taking $1,300 out of the pocket of each inhabitant on the planet. What for? To create an additional real growth in GDP equal to zero. A great example of the results of the state's "do-goodism".

> We are creating money out of thin air [...] we have lost control.
>
> Ron Paul

We are told that fresh measures are needed to stabilise the markets, house prices, and so forth. "Stabilise" here really means "prevent supply and demand from working", since these policies do nothing but manipulate prices. QE policies seek to recreate or maintain the same bubbles that brought us into the crisis. That is what is meant by "stabilise".

This is not a new policy. Nero and other Roman emperors already cheated the monetary system by issuing coins made from a combination of gold and silver years back. In 1715, John Law proposed to reduce France's excessive debt by printing currency so as to buy shares from a business called Mississippi Company, convinced that the American state would become a garden of growth. It created a bubble which, upon bursting, brought down the currency and the markets.

What happened after the collapse? Was anything learnt from it? No. The situation was repeated in 1790 in France with the "assignats" (paper currency printed uncontrollably) and also ended in disaster.

Unfortunately, we didn't learn and the policy of creating money out of thin air continued with the Weimar Republic in 1920. There are other examples, and they have always ended badly.

Doesn't all this ring a bell when you hear that the ECB is going to "purchase unlimited bonds", or that the Federal Reserve "will continue buying bonds and mortgage instruments indefi- nitely"? Today, we are repeating the same practice and, as before, we are told there is no risk and that everything is under control. They say that this time it's different.

And we get angry because Germany is unwilling to mon- etise debt (meaning, to print money). A country that seems to have learnt from its mistakes is deemed the "bad guy".

One thing that never ceases to amaze me is how unrestrain- edly QE is hailed and applauded as something good, when it only benefits the markets and inflation, above all in commodi- ties and gold. When this happens, the press will look for a culprit in OPEC or speculators to explain the rise in commodi- ties, but the reason is that the investor rushes to protect himself from the destruction of wealth following the massive printing of money, from the plundering of savers to maintain interest rates at an all-time low and from the risk of inflation. We are undergoing a process that is attempting to re-inflate the bubbles, be they in the financial markets (stock market bubble) or in the housing markets (through "bad banks", bonds and mortgage pools, and so forth).

Even though indiscriminate monetary policy is proven to create large imbalances, even though people see how their disposable income disappears, even though we see we can't make ends meet and that everything is much dearer (while "official inflation" is supposedly "very low"), despite all this we are made to believe that without this it "would have been worse".

As the Kinks sang: "Give the people what they want." Well, now they have it.

In general, the problem of QE is simple: when the patient is exhausted, adrenaline shots only cause spasms. Yet in the context of the economy, these adrenaline shots cost ordinary people – and future generations – hundreds of billions, and the additional units of debt that are injected into the system no longer produce positive marginal effects.

It's that simple. A problem of debt created over decades is not resolved in days. You don't get something out of nothing, and there are no magic formulas.

The impact of quantitative easing in emerging markets

With cheap money created by the US Federal Reserve, we also see big volatility in dollar-based economies.

The risk in emerging markets is not only lower than expected growth in Brazil, Mexico, India or China. The big dilemma is what markets call "a sudden stop": an abrupt disruption in the flow of capital investment.

One of the consequences of monetary stimulus in recent years has been extreme inflation in risky assets. The US exports inflation to semi-dollar-based economies and emerging markets, and some of the favourite investments throughout QE times have been emerging market bonds. So much so that we have seen very low-quality bond issuers access the market at extremely low rates.

With the prospect of the Federal Reserve reducing its stimulus in May 2014, markets saw a wave of unprecedented withdrawal of capital, particularly from emerging markets.

- The reserves of the central banks of emerging countries lost $81 billion, but financing needs increased by 7% and current account deficits were giving alarm signals.
- Excessive inflation and the collapse of local currencies made current account deficits soar in Latin American countries.
- The access to cheap credit and dollars and easy money created excessive liquidity for emerging economies, around $10 billion per month, according to the estimates of several investment banks. And this excessive liquidity had become a new norm. Unfortunately, periods of excess liquidity were not used to reduce risk and strengthen economies but are assumed to be new paradigms of normality... until the tide turns.

The impact on economic growth and stability in emerging countries could be very relevant. The combination of high inflation, current account deficits and loss of dollar reserves by central banks has never been a winning one. And the three variables deteriorate very quickly.

Many of these countries and their companies have debt in dollars and now hold less US currency to meet their commitments.

The economic instability of many of these countries was not a topic of discussion at the Fed until the world became concerned about the brutal collapse of the Indian rupee against the dollar in 2014.

A "sudden stop" has global effects. It has a significant impact on European banks, heavily exposed to Latin America, and multinational companies of the old continent, as it begins to glimpse its way out of the recession, and very important direct consequences for British and American banks, because of their exposure to Asia and Africa. But above all, it creates challenges for developing countries, with increasing refinancing needs, if they cannot access the capital markets after the boom years of the Fed "money helicopter".

For the EU, this is not such bad news. Capital outflows from developing countries go to "low-risk countries" in Europe. Financial asset rotation out of risky assets into defensive countries has always benefited the EU and the US.

How to avoid "a sudden stop"? The best way to avoid a huge meltdown in developing countries is to do just what the Fed is doing. Dip its toe in the water but not much, say "Yes, we will taper QE" and then watch the consequences.

It can be a small one-off shock or a snowball, but a "sudden stop" is not irrelevant.

CHAPTER NINETEEN

LIES AND MISTAKES OF
THE DEBT CRISIS

From 2007 to 2011, we lived what I call the "spoilt brat tantrum". By then, I was already writing for *El Confidencial* and had warned, along with dozens of analysts and journalists around the world, of snowballing debt and the exponential risk it was creating. Peter Schiff and Ron Paul were accused of being alarmists. How dare you spoil the party while the music is still playing and everyone is having fun!

The warnings signs were there. The ratings had been stretched to the limit, the banks' results were showing an increase in arrears and debt, corporate profit margins were beginning to slide and GDP growth was not being reflected in improved cash figures. Market saturation was being felt in all areas.

In 2009, I warned on my blog that we should start "praying for demand to start up dramatic growth again, because if not, the bill at the end is going to be immense". In 2012, I wrote that "the hole that we are creating is sustainable, because the cost of the plan 'to keep growing and growing' will be paid by our grandchildren."

However, states resorted to whinging like spoilt brats who had been caught up to no good. "It wasn't me", "It's not fair",

"You did more" and "If you don't give it to me, I'll scream and stamp my feet." While many of us were warning that the credit cake was shrinking and difficulties to obtain money would only increase, many countries and operators invoked their right to continue digging the debt hole opened up over the last decade.

We saw appeals from many quarters to "forget the deficit" (more debt), to safeguard social rights (more debt), to pursue growth policies (more debt) and to default (meltdown). I wondered how we could be so selfish as to cheer while we spent the money of future generations under the illusory promise that "we'll grow again".

The greatest deception of the last decade was to call what was really debt "growth", and today call "austerity" what is little more than a contained glut. The term "austerity" is just a slight budgetary restraint, a consequence of earlier reckless spending. Think how well off we would be today had we gone on strike in 2005, while the state was multiplying our debt two-fold, with a huge banner proclaiming, "We will not put our grandchildren at risk."

Debt matters – a lot. Above all on account of its volume: €3.2 trillion additional debt in the eurozone since 2002, and an ECB with a balance that already exceeds €2 trillion.

> *The work of a politician is not to reduce debt but to look for fun and creative ways to hide it.*
>
> Trader's comment

Eight myths about the crisis

Let's examine a few of the biggest myths about the crisis:

"Now is the time for the state to spend."
Solving debt with more debt. We forget that when we pay current expenditure with debt our children will be the ones to foot the bill, with interest.

"Our problem is not public debt, but private debt."

Governments spend between 10 and 20% more than what they collect in tax revenues. No company finds itself in that situation. Comparing private and public debt as a percentage of GDP paints an incorrect picture. Public debt is the problem. Hence the risk of needing a bailout. Because there would be no real demand for this debt.

On the other hand, the argument of drawing a comparison between private debt and public debt is simply absurd. They are entirely different concepts. To begin with, private debt is supported by assets and profits.

Private debt is freely contracted. It's repaid with capital injections, divestitures and free cash flow. If the company cannot pay, it goes bankrupt, its assets are sold and its debts settled.

Public debt is mandatorily imposed. It is repaid with more taxes and more cuts, and if it isn't paid it ruins ordinary people. Thus, although the amount of current private debt is larger than public debt, the first is quoted with a much lower risk premium than that of sovereign debt. The differences are important.

"Debt is illegitimate."

Leaders of the left in Europe are champions of calls for "auditing debt", calling debt illegitimate and restructuring it (defaulting), and have the audacity to describe as "illegitimate" the commitments that have been generated under democracy and, especially between 2008 and 2011, with the consent of all the parties and trade unions. Above all, they live in cloud cuckoo land if they believe that a default would have no effect on future access to credit, the risk premium and the "social rights of ordinary people".

"If the European Central Bank had lent to peripherals at zero interest, there would be no deficit problem today."

No, there would be a bankrupt Europe. If all the states had been financed with zero or extremely low interest, the public spending spiral would have accelerated even more. The cost of debt is essential for preventing wastage, in the same way a person revises and moderates his spending when credit card costs rise. Remember that Europe has borrowed three trillion euros in five years and that the balance sheet of the ECB rose steeply to some €2 trillion by 2013. Had all the EU states been financed at a zero interest rate, the wasteful spending spree would have not only continued but also multiplied. And the real problem of the primary deficit (the deficit excluding the cost of debt) would remain unresolved.

Such huge mountains of debt would be passed on to the ECB, which is funded with taxes from the citizens of the EU. Furthermore, the central bank would have imposed conditions on the most indebted countries, thus making cuts and tax hikes equally necessary. We would have broken into the piggy bank in any case and we would also have created systemic risk across Europe.

The eurozone had a real debt:GDP ratio exceeding 90% at a time when interest rates were extremely low. Can you imagine how much debt the EU countries would have accrued if, moreover, they had been given free rein? Inflation and taxes would have created the same problems for the eurozone it experienced after the massive credit growth of 2001–2008, which exceeded all stimulus made in the US relative to GDP.

The funding of states at negligible rates gives rise to unfair competition and undermines the investment process. What's more, it provides brilliant conditions for the blank chequebook approach to public finances that gave Spain such white elephants as the statues of Castellón.

"There's no growth without debt."

While people demonstrate for more debt and more spending and the so-called policies of "debt for growth" abound, the proof that debt doesn't equate with growth is borne out by a study by Carmen Reinhart and Kenneth Rogoff of the Peterson Institute, titled *A Decade of Debt*, according to which the economies of both advanced and emerging countries that have experienced the most growth in GDP per capita are those with the lowest debt:GDP ratios (less than 30%).

"The European Central Bank must inject funds into the banks in order to reduce risk."

Quantitative easing without fiscal adjustment is a ticking time bomb, because it will only work at very specific moments and not when there are structural deficits. We have already seen its ineffectiveness with LTROs (long-term refinancing operations) and similar projects. Debt is not solved with more debt, and the risk of contagion increases rather than reduces. When people say, "The ECB, not the taxpayers, must bail out the banks", where do they think the money from the central bank comes from? From the taxpayer. Do they believe that this debt will not be met with current or future taxes?

"If we lower the deficit, the risk premium will drop."

Lowering the deficit only reduces the amount of additional debt. If I owed you €1,000, and then said I was going to owe you €1,200 but later lowered it to "only" €1,100, as a creditor you wouldn't be at all happy. The risk premium gauges the surplus return required of sluggish economies that cannot repay their debt. Slightly lowering the inability to repay doesn't lower its premium. The only real solution is to lower the absolute debt, sell off assets and attract capital and stop borrowing to pay off interest on loans. Too often cuts and tax rises only cover financial cost. A problem of liquidity that is on its way to being a problem of solvency is only solved by reducing expenditure to the level of the previous year's revenue – not by praying for earnings to rise.

We still fail to see that a debt problem cannot be solved by being repackaged and concealed. And we continue to forget that the risk is not dissipated by accumulation, it simply spreads. We seem not to have learnt anything from the subprime mortgage crisis, or from the mergers of savings banks. Europe and Spain must look for a way to create growth without overwhelming the taxpayer with more borrowing.

"Taxes must be raised."

A tax hike would get in the way of creating new business. The tax burden in the OECD averaged 35%, according to Eurostat. Indirect taxation is also higher, with hydrocarbons, regional and local taxes at the top. Even if we made use of what some people believe amounts to €12 billion in "tax evasion and additional taxes" – an exaggerated sum – we would not be able to reduce absolute debt. We would continue to create primary and total deficit.

The UK Coalition government's formula of "business is great" plus low taxes has worked. By lowering SME and self-employed taxes, the UK not only increased its revenue collection by £24 billion but also reduced the unemployment rate to 7%, even with net immigration increasing.

Tax revenues in Europe have not collapsed because of fraud or the black economy but because of the enormous dependency on government spending on civil works, a bubble of overcapacity used to artificially inflate GDP. Instead of creating good conditions for economic growth and with them generate more tax revenues, Europe shot itself in the foot by creating a tax system that discourages investment.

Instead of considering that spending must be adapted to the economic cycles and that prosperity always had come from saving, we start to think that an excessive spending problem will be fixed with more spending.

Some additional concepts need clarifying:

The European debt crisis was not the same as the American, British or Japanese ones: it was worse.

The utilisation of financial resources (debt) for bureaucratic and low-productivity expenses, together with high taxation, are what most set the European crisis apart from its American,

British or Japanese counterparts. The European model redistributes resources to non-productive elements. Bureaucracy is disguised as social expenditure.

Unrestrained public debt matters, not only because it is paid for with taxes and cuts or becomes non-payment but also because it has huge impact on the financial situation of the European banks. These would need €100 billion, according to the IMF, to achieve the minimum capitalisation required by the European Union itself.

The use of those financial resources matters very much, as it has led to a tax burden that already accounts for 44% of GDP, a tax-revenue voracity that does nothing but increase and continue to destroy employment and businesses.

Debt is not capital. It's debt. And it costs money.

The problem of the debt crisis is that the practice of hiding debts under the carpet makes us believe that debt is capital.

I read in December 2012 about someone who said that "Germany is stealing the capital of the southern countries". What capital? Almost all of it is debt. All economists, from Keynes to Hayek to Marx, warned of the illusion of valuing the accumulation of debt over debt as if it were "capital". Here in Europe we have betrayed all the principles of credit build-up.

Rather than mitigate problems, the accumulation of debt deepens them.

Accumulating deficit is like trying to climb out of a hole by burrowing deeper. When you spend 20 to 25% more than you earn, the only solution is to stop digging (spending), because higher taxation only achieves less investment, less employment and less work.

Intervention in the debt market prevents businesses from gaining access to credit.

If an intervention in the market takes place, and states receive extremely generous yet unjustified terms, the banks that should be providing credit for investment will simply not lend to companies. It's as if you were a school and you had to choose between granting a place to a boy who has the answers to all the exams but is a dunce and another who doesn't have the answers but is bright. The choice is clear. This is what we discussed above, the "crowding out" effect, whereby the state monopolises credit.

Behind every central bank there are private investors and taxes for you to pay.

A central bank that becomes a Roach Motel insect trap (where nothing that goes in comes out) is a bomb about to go off, and without private investors willing to take risks because the economy is in a slump, the taxpayer will end up paying for it. This goes for any central bank, be it the Bank of England or the Federal Reserve. In any event, you will pay in inflation, loss of currency value or in taxes. There is no alternative.

I recall what a fixed-income manager remarked about the measures from the ECB: "A decisive solution, with non-existent money, to purchase debt that will not be repaid using an untested mechanism."

Regardless who the lender entity is – be it the ECB, the European Financial Stability Facility (EFSF), or its replacement, the European Stability Mechanism (ESM) – it in turn has to finance itself in the secondary market, with domestic or foreign capital, sovereign wealth funds and so on. Investors who risk their own money or that of their countries' feel considerable uncertainty when they see the legal structure, the mandates and the limits of these mechanisms being discussed and redesigned almost every month. Therefore, none of these organisations will enter the benchmarks used by funds to decide where to invest. In short, by threatening the legal structures that underpin these mechanisms, we also scare away the investors we need most. Would you invest in a fund that has to change its prospectus every month?

Monetising debt isn't a panacea: you pay for it anyway.

If monetising debt (printing money) were the solution, Zimbabwe and Argentina would be the world's most successful countries.

This doesn't work without financial credibility. Printing currency leads to inflation (the silent tax), less disposable income and less growth, which we are experiencing every day. It steals from the saver to perpetuate the expenditure of an indebted state.

And monetising debt, as we have seen in the United States and the United Kingdom, doesn't prevent budget cuts or reduce the need to undertake reforms. In fact, the adjustments are extremely harsh because the amount of debt outstanding becomes unsustainable, as we have seen with the fiscal cliff in the United States.

Deficit is not a right, and debt is not a blessing.

I heard a member of the Spanish Autonomous Government of Galicia demanding its "right to run up the same deficit as that of the Spanish state". Deficit is not a right, never mind an accumulative right of each state, each region, each town council, each district... because at the end of this chain, who pays? You do.

If you believe that the market generates unaffordable costs, don't saturate it.

If I don't like the lenders, I wouldn't go asking them for dosh every day. If you want to combat the supposed dictatorship of the markets, don't let yourself become steeped in debt. Let's not spend 15–20% more than we earn in order to grant subsidies and pay for politically motivated spending.

One cannot demand both more credit and less credit responsibility. We are making a huge blunder if we think that by shirking our responsibilities to service our debt we will receive more funding. The lender has an ugly habit of wanting his money returned and with interest, and if our credibility suffers, the funding will disappear or the cost of borrowing will skyrocket.

In late 2012, the balance sheet of the ECB exceeded 30% of the eurozone's GDP, as compared with 20% of the Federal Reserve or the Bank of England. The countries that contribute to the ECB were also heavily indebted, and the number of "taxpayers" declined as the number of countries with economic problems increased. The worst thing is that by resigning oneself to a bailout, one resigns oneself to enslavement, to mortgage.

Bitcoin: Free currency, bubble or Ponzi scheme?

Bitcoin is the beginning of something great: a currency without a government, something necessary and imperative

Nassim Taleb

In 2014, years after the massive money printing actions throughout the OECD, there were many articles about Bitcoin, the so-called virtual currency that increased in price more than 100 times in eleven months, then collapsed and continued its extremely volatile journey.

My opinion is simple: Bitcoin is not a reality; it's an expectation, and therefore its price evolution depends on its getting deployed globally and clarifying doubts about its role as a method of payment and "storage of value".

Bitcoin is a start-up currency. Its initial appeal is undeniable. A method of payment where states cannot interfere in the money supply, and where investors can find a safe haven from the assault on the saver that is the increased financial repression imposed by governments and central banks. Sure, but my doubts come when the haven is virtual, and therefore always subject to hacker attacks. In addition, there's the risk of a confiscatory reaction from states if it reaches a "dangerously high" implementation. "Free" currencies tend to end up being abolished or confiscated.

For now, Bitcoin is not a currency; it is an exchange network. Like a financial asset, a future or a derivative. Unlike legal tender currencies, no one is forced to accept it as a method of payment. It is not dissimilar to a barter coupon. You accept it as payment for goods and services just the same way as you use something that is perceived as valuable by both parties, buyer and seller, be it a watch, a car or Bitcoin. As such, its value is based on a generalised perception of scarcity, future demand, liquidity and quality as a means of determining what currency, good or service it can be exchanged for in the future.

As a "storage of value" asset it has some similarities with a gold ETF (exchange tracker fund), but it is massively more volatile... and virtual. Therefore, it is subject to extreme changes of perception with a supply and potential demand that is difficult to estimate.

However, it has no real similarity with physical gold, having no history of transactions in times of extreme crisis. Everyone knows that gold can be exchanged for goods and services in case of a global catastrophe. Nobody knows yet how you create virtual storage of value.

To be a currency, Bitcoin must go a long way in implementation, and be accepted globally for large and meaningful commercial transactions.

I finally received a good report with a detailed analysis (*Bitcoin: A First Assessment* by Bank of America Merrill Lynch) that seeks to clarify the risks and opportunities of this virtual phenomenon.

According to Merrill Lynch, assuming Bitcoin becomes a widespread means of payment for transfers and e-commerce, an approach to its valuation could be reached through the addition of:

- the average capitalisation of established means of payment such as Western Union, MoneyGram and Euronet
- the expectation that Bitcoin could capture 10% of global e-commerce, and the US investment bank estimates this at $5 billion

that is, around $9.5 billion capitalisation, below the market level, which stands above $13 billion.

The first part of the valuation analysis seems appropriate in a conservative scenario, but some could say that Bitcoin, having the benefit of a restricted supply, should capitalise above Western Union.

But it is the second part of the sum which is more complex to analyse. To reach $5 billion, Merrill Lynch assumes that Bitcoin would accumulate 10% of online residential sales in the US, and extrapolates it to the rest of the world. In the US the total e-commerce market is $224 billion and the domestic sector (households) accounts for approximately $10 billion, of which 10% would potentially be absorbed by Bitcoin. If we assume that the US is close to 20% of global GDP and a similar degree of penetration of both trade and online commerce of Bitcoin in the world, Merrill's analysts arrive at the figure of $5 billion capitalisation. However, that number could be much higher if we included companies using Bitcoin aggressively. If we add companies with 10% implementation, this part could reach $50 billion capitalisation, assuming other electronic payment penetration levels.

Such an assessment would indicate that Bitcoin is either nearly 30% above its fundamental value, or up to 420% undervalued, depending on the penetration assumptions.

That is the dilemma of analysing Bitcoin, to understand the ability to penetrate markets which today are huge and where a space can be generated for this method of payment without falling into the risks of:

- Being a threat to states and their control over currency and the money supply. In a world where central banks and governments have made financial repression the last resort to support excessive debt spending, the use of legislation to attack any means that threatens their main weapon of economic policy should not be underestimated. Bitcoin, even in the middle of the valuation range, would be far from becoming a "problem" like that.

- Confiscation of assets Roosevelt-style as we have seen in the past with gold, and other paradigms of government actions to steal the savings of investors in "safe havens". Being a virtual asset makes this very difficult, but not impossible.

For Bitcoin to be a bubble, global electronic commerce estimates should be much lower than the current maximum capitalisation (i.e. the perception of demand unachievable in a fairly conservative analysis). When we consider the current sales trends of global online commerce, that risk disappears.

In addition, to be a bubble, Bitcoin should meet the requirement of having a rapid and increasing supply well above demand. Bitcoin supply is limited to 21 million by 2140.

To be a Ponzi scheme it should meet the following criteria:

- That profitability granted to existing holders of Bitcoin is guaranteed by additional coins purchased by new investors, i.e. to make the number of new investors constantly increase. That is not the case: the valuation of Bitcoin is fixed by demand and supply generated by a multitude of buyers and sellers, and sellers have no false guarantee or allegedly safe return.
- That price dynamics is uniform, opaque and controlled by a single operator, providing a false sense of security, i.e. it only goes up until new buyers stop joining the pyramid scheme and it explodes. Bitcoin buyers are aware of the volatility and possibility of selling at a loss. Bitcoin has seen huge rises in price and massive falls. It behaves more like a financial start-up, an asset where the price is being checked every day according to the potential supply and demand.

Therefore, it is not like a Ponzi scheme.

Bitcoin, for valuation purposes, is equivalent to a tech start-up or a junior explorer-miner. Its value only transpires when it begins to dispel doubts about its implementation as a combination of means of payment and safe haven.

To achieve the potential and penetration needed to justify much higher prices, there are two things to look for:

• The enormous volatility, with moves of 30–40% in one day, makes it difficult for large companies and massive consumers to accept it quickly. Volatility itself prevents its penetration into the mass market. To be a universally accepted means of payment it should have similar levels of volatility to those established currencies or gold. That's why I say it's still not a currency but a volatile financial asset.

• The length and quality of exchange. Bitcoin has a major advantage – supply is limited – and to avoid manipulation by a bank or state, there is no centralised validation system (clearing) that is why each transaction is analysed and delayed, to avoid double counting. Well, for large transactions this means some time, which greatly limits the mass deployment in companies and trade. Furthermore, several of the servers have been hacked. One such exchange, Bitcoinica, lost 18,547 bitcoins after a cyber-attack. BIPS in Europe lost 1,195 after a security issue.

When transactions are immediate, safe and not subject to huge volatility, the valuation of Bitcoin could start to make sense.

There are still many issues to clarify. If you find it difficult to understand the phenomenon, it is best to avoid it, not ride a wave dependent on variables with huge fluctuations.

What I find interesting is that Bitcoin shows that more people are scared and looking for ways to get out of the vicious circle of financial repression and devaluation of currencies. The implementation of an "intervention-free currency" or means of payment can only be positive. And, if Bitcoin or any other free currency ends up being widely used, it may restore sanity to those governments that engage in this race of currency destruction they want to sell us as "social" and that in reality is just a massive transfer of wealth from savers to the indebted states.

Ten myths about tax havens

Tax evasion and money laundering are big problems. But those problems are solved by employing a strong legal and penal system not by attacking tax competition and foreign investment. It is not a coincidence to see a debate on tax havens at the same time as we live through the greatest financial repression since the seventies, when political spending in OECD countries soars to record highs. Tax havens are the new scapegoat.

In my opinion, the main mistakes in this debate are:

1. **Tax heavens or tax hells?** The debate throughout Europe starts with a translation error that is not accidental, or irrelevant. Many European countries translate *tax haven* as "tax heaven". It's a very important semantic difference. It is important, because that translation error occurs, not by chance either, in countries where the most interventionist policies are implemented. The assets of banks in tax havens have increased by approximately $10 trillion since 2001. According to Harvard University, the increase in these assets happens almost always after the tax burden increases with about twelve months' difference. That is, the movement of capital out of tax hells comes *after* tax increases. It is not the cause of these tax increases, as some want to tell us, but a consequence of financial repression.

2. **They shelter illegal funds.** Another myth is putting everything under the "illegal" banner. In late 2010, according to Tax Justice, the fifty largest banks managed $12.1 trillion in assets offshore. This is known data, with operations that are legal, either from investments or corporate accounts. The vast majority comes from companies with multinational trade agreements seeking two objectives. One is to grow and develop their activities in the world without incurring double taxation, which creates many more social benefits, employment and wealth than capital controls. Another is to safeguard funds

from complex countries, e.g. Venezuela. Thanks to tax havens companies have been able to avoid instituted capital controls and confiscation of part of their investments in those countries.

3. **Billions of lost tax revenue.** According to the study *Do tax havens divert economic activity?* empirical evidence shows that tax shelters do not reduce economic activity in high-tax countries, but actually increase it.[17] Because assets are reinvested in sovereign debt, stocks and business projects in OECD countries with high taxation. Also, economic activity not only increased with the growth of tax shelters but also benefited mostly Western countries, as a large part of the money that is protected in tax havens from global totalitarian regimes is reinvested in the US, Europe and UK. This is an important factor, because we tend to forget the amount of money from honest citizens looking to take their money out of repressive dictatorial regimes.

4. **They are in exotic locations.** What is a tax haven? Nobody in Spain, for example, complained when its companies conquered the world buying assets and deducting goodwill from the tax base. Our benefits are always tax "reforms" and the others are "evasion". Who decides what is a good or bad tax territory? Delaware, Nevada, Wyoming, Luxembourg, Malta, Cyprus, Andorra, Jersey, Ireland, Lichtenstein, Switzerland or even Navarra... all have distinct and significant tax benefits. Is Cayman bad and Luxembourg good? Why?

5. **They generate unfair tax competition.** We talk about tax harmonisation as a panacea. Except that harmonisation is not the echo of the Beach Boys singing *Our Prayer*, it means raising taxes on everyone. A confiscatory state never has enough. And it does not save in prosperous times. It is precisely the tax competition of different countries that prevents

---

[17] http://deepblue.lib.umich.edu/bitstream/handle/2027.42/39145/1024.pdf?sequence=1

you from working for the government until September, as happened a few decades ago. In 1979, the average personal income tax in the OECD in the top range exceeded 67% and the corporate income tax was 50%, plus there were taxes on capital of all kinds. Was the state more efficient before and countries enjoyed greater wealth? No. Today, thanks to openness and tax competition, we have much lower taxes.

6. **Competing with tax havens is a race to zero.** No, it's not. Tax havens have levels of public spending that stand at around 25% of GDP. That, in itself, precludes the race to zero. In any case, the race must be to provide services that citizens view as adequate and of quality. As Will Rogers said, "The best that can be said of the tax system is that, thank God, we don't have the amount of government that we pay for."

7. **We can eliminate tax havens.** There will always be tax competition. The same as in the seventies when France was a tax haven for the British, there will always be a sovereign country to attract capital efficiently. Or do we really think Brussels will impose its tax system on China–Hong Kong, Singapore, Dubai, etc.? How? By cutting trade? Please. Capital restrictions led us to the worst recession since the Second World War … and, above all, they did not work. Tax evasion and the underground economy in Europe in the seventies were higher than today in terms of GDP. Another thing I love is the issue of transparency. According to the World Bank, most of the major tax shelters have better corporate governance and transparency than some European countries.

8. **They finance terrorism and money laundering.** The Institute of Governance at the University of Basel made a very detailed analysis of countries with a high risk of terrorist financing and money laundering, and out of 28 countries identified only one that could be considered a "tax haven". Money laundering and terrorism will always exist, unfortunately, and what needs to be done is to attack the source and apply strong criminal penalties.

9. **The perception that tax havens are no risk.** Investing offshore is expensive, costing millions of dollars in commissions, and it is also complex and risky. Very risky. Why do people do it then? Because we have turned our countries into tax hells that pursue predatory policies.

10. **The argument which states that without tax havens there would not have been a crisis.** We are overwhelmed with figures. Billions and billions. Of course, all estimates. And also – this is very important – we confuse assets with liabilities and capital accumulated with annual profit. I use two figures: $8 trillion, according to the Boston Consulting Group, and $21 trillion, according to Tax Justice, which has a tad of interest in inflating the figure. But it does not matter. Assume that these figures are true and that all belonged to OECD citizens and assume a 20% tax, to be generous, which, of course, would be applied only once. What do we find? That with all proceeds we would not cover the deficit in the last three years of the OECD. If the US taxed 20% what some say American companies hold in foreign accounts, it would not cover the 2012 deficit.

The current crisis is due to government mismanagement of bubble-period revenues that they assumed would be eternal. Tax revenues in the EU do not collapse because of selfishness but because investment conditions are atrocious and taxes too high for people to invest.

Globalisation, free movement of capital and trade have made it possible to enjoy the rights that many now claim. Tax havens do not thrive when there is a fair and low tax environment. Returning to capital controls and the nanny state will lead to equality in misery.

The best policy against tax havens is not to become a tax hell.

CHAPTER TWENTY

ECONOMIC LIBERTY AND AUSTERITY

These days, there is a school of thought whose underlying argument is that the state's economic decisions are by nature well meaning and so we should forgive it for its errors. The interventionists expect you to feel cornered and believe there is no solution but to yield to the government's demands. And the worst of these demands, the most outrageous, is that which defends the idea that we must cede more of our economic freedom to allow the very states that have landed us in this crisis to bring us out of it by setting up new government-run organisations.

With this in mind, I defend individual economic freedom.

The incentives and risk-versus-benefit ratios of states and their agents are not aligned with yours or mine as citizens. It's not a matter of eliminating the state, which performs essential functions. It's about preventing the state's abuse. The optimist's theory, which holds that the state always acts according to general interest, should not mean it is handed a blank cheque to repeat the same mistake over and over again. A bad manager has his funds withdrawn, is put on the dole or even sent to prison. However, a bad public-sector administrator, once he's lost the elections, is appointed to a board.

It's incongruous that states and their central banks, who have indebted their economies to choking point, tell you they need even more economic powers – as if they had little – to the detriment of families and businesses, who are the only ones to have acted prudently and adapted, as I have, to the crisis. And they make use of fear to get you to voluntarily surrender your last ounce of economic freedom. We are told there is no alternative other than to repeat what has already been done once again. States must convince you that if expenditure is reduced, or taxes lowered, we will destroy our economy. In doing so, they merely kick the can farther down the road.

> *A government big enough to give you everything you*
> *want is strong enough to take everything you have.*
>
> Thomas Jefferson

The solution is simple. Let some insolvent banks fail and have their assets auctioned off. The system must be cleaned up instead of postponing the solution and making the hole even bigger. We have been putting off a response to this question since 2008. If we had taken action then, we would be discussing a strong recovery by now.

Any other solution is like giving a drunk more alcohol. This not only fails to help, but its immediate effect dissipates faster each time.

In the words of the great composer Jim Steinman, "The future ain't what it used to be." That's precisely the problem.

Austerity and growth

> *Inflation won't resolve the problem created by*
> *parasitic relations. The more state subsidies there*
> *are, the less economic growth there will be.*
>
> Robert Reich

Many economists oppose austerity. One of them is Paul Krugman, who calls for more spending, more intervention by governments and central banks, wage cuts to boost competitiveness and massive tax increases to offset the expenditure generated by this "stabilisation" process.

However, a growing number of investors and analysts argue that these measures are futile and unjustified. Over recent years, we have witnessed the continued failure of the New Keynesian policies of kicking the can down the road. John Maynard Keynes himself defended saving in periods of growth, but governments always forget to do it. I believe Keynes would probably have criticised this "eternal stimulus" for having made the norm what was supposed to be an exceptional measure. These policies are also criticised by many neoclassical economists. In fact, many experts in economic analysis who observe the negative effects of the current aggressive model on a daily basis are beginning to put forward an alternative. This alternative comes from the Austrian School, with authorities of the likes of Friedrich Hayek, Ludwig Von Mises and George Reisman.

The Austrian School is a school of economic thought that emphasises subjectivism, radical uncertainty, time, liquidity, dynamic adjustment and the irreducible information problems of state intervention as the pillars of their analytical framework.

To my mind, the most relevant aspects of the Austrian School are: its defence of the importance of freedom as a check and balance in price formations, the non-neutrality of money and the theory that interest rates and profits are determined from the interaction of different operators with different marginal productivities. And, last but not least, it shows above all that when states and central banks intervene in economic relations they have a disruptive impact on the system's spring cleaning, giving rise to "boom and bust" processes. Despite my neoclassical and Keynesian background, I found that the

Austrian School's observations really drive home the damaging effects of intervention policies.

I will summarise a talk I delivered in London, Dallas and Austin titled "Austerity works", in which I try to demonstrate from my own experience that the well-meaning formulas which the advocates of public spending promulgate "to kick-start domestic demand" are based upon several misconceptions, which are particularly evident in Europe:

• The fall in private investment is an unjustified anomaly, not the result of the conditions of overcapacity and low growth forecast.
• European governments would spend taxpayers' money more efficiently and prudently than the private sector.
• Governments centre their investment criteria on seeking adequate profitability-controlled costs and good management.
• Government decisions to invest and spend are compatible with private initiatives and the free market (when they are not, because they interfere in price formation and competition).
• Bad public investment decisions can always be offset with more taxes and growth.

The vast majority of "growth" plans approved in Europe have been shown to yield poor returns – on average most are loss-making since 2005, according to our internal analysis – as well as interfering in the competitive process by protecting low-productivity sectors or those in decline, and maintaining semi-governmental subsidised companies on life-support. In fact, in many cases, "investments" by European governments have held back economic recovery, owing to the debt and overcapacity they leave in their wake. For this reason, it's necessary to tackle the debt problem in terms of spending, in other words: austerity.

Europe is not exactly undertaking an austerity drive, but a cost-containment process, which is very moderate in the cases of Spain and Britain. Lowering the "deficit" from 8 to 6% is not austerity; it's budgetary prudence. It's not the same to reduce debt as it is to prevent it from rising.

The first argument usually used to attack austerity programmes is to compare them with what happened in the thirties, when the result of these measures worsened the crisis. But we overlook the differences.

- In the thirties, austerity measures were combined with protectionism, a mix that our leaders should avoid. In a globalised world, it would be difficult to see the fierce protectionism of the United States of the thirties. However, interventionism is on the rise in Europe, but not alarmingly so.
- In the thirties, interest rates were extremely high and the financial capacity of systems which were subject to government interventions was very limited. This is not the case today.
- In the thirties, there was no globalisation, which today allows exporting businesses to benefit from growth in the emerging economies and facilitates the free circulation of global capital.

As I previously mentioned, we should also recall debt saturation. We have saturated the dubiously "beneficial" effect of spending. We are not just talking about the billions thrown at circus and arts cities, unused airports, infrastructures multiplied and subsidised by sunk costs. The problem is that all this spending was not underpinned by equivalent earnings. There was no return on invested capital, which left behind only non-existent value, yet debt must be covered with earnings from other, productive, activities. In other words, the "infrastructures and subsidies" are not only wasteful, but the debt they produce is taken from more profitable activities. Lastly, they create "non-investment": no one dares to put a penny into an economy where the taxes that generate productive investment are allocated to funding unproductive wastage.

People accept this type of spending because they view useless infrastructures as an asset: "I have an empty airport that doesn't generate earnings... but I have an airport." By seeing things in this light, they forget the negative and even exclusionary effect of this useless kind of infrastructure and the debt it generates on other productive activities.

Why austerity works:

- It diverts financial resources from unproductive activities to productive ones. Today, large parts of the financial resources at the European banks' disposal are used to buy public debt and finance local government spending. It is the "crowding out" effect of a state that already accounts for over 40% of the eurozone's economy. If the state stops monopolising the available credit and spending it on unproductive activities, investor activity will return as well as the funding for this investment.

- It speeds up the transition to a more productive economy. It's no coincidence that productivity falls when public spending increases. Most public spending goes on stimulus plans to subsidise and prop up both industries in decline (e.g. the mining and automotive industries) and activities with extremely low output (e.g. construction and civil engineering), and it monopolises financial resources which are sorely needed for high-productivity investment. If governments put a halt to propping up these unproductive companies and sectors, they will attract investment in high-productivity areas. If not, this capital will move to more attractive countries.

- It helps to create real jobs, rather than subsidised ones. When the state spends on pointless companies and investments that give no return, it's not creating employment but subsidising it by borrowing money. And this comes out of the productive worker's pocket and taxes from profitable companies... until the taxpayers' money runs out and the pyramid collapses.

- It creates GDP, rather than whittles it away. The increase in financial expenditure stifles recovery and gives rise to tax increases that discourage consumption and investment, as well as drive away capital. Austerity does not just curb payment of useless subsidies; it also attracts capital and reduces the loss of tax revenue by bringing in new investment.

We must get out of this spending spiral, of favours owed, of protectionism and subsidies that prop up unproductive sectors and block innovation and investment in growth. Spain did this in the past, on several occasions, so I can't see why it can't do it again.

In my book *Journey to Economic Freedom* (Deusto, 2013) I devote a chapter to the mistakes in economic policies of many countries in the European Union that copied France: stagnation, high taxation and lack of reforms. In order to maintain at all costs a hypertrophied state and bloated administrations, funds are spent on useless schemes at the expense of those who generate wealth.

At the smallest hint of a recovery we see that countries, instead of continuing with reforms, decide to relax and fall back into recession.

The economy is still not recovering enough in Europe, the transmission belt for monetary policy remains broken, debt, both in relative and absolute terms, continues to grow and employment is not improving.

First, credit to the private sector still has not improved because all available credit is crowded out by government debt, making the financial system more risky and therefore more fragile against any sovereign risk.

Wages are still falling, and to think that forcing Germany to stimulate its domestic demand will have a ripple effect on the periphery is wrong empirically, because the multiplier effect of attracting foreign capital and direct financial investment is three times higher than that of any internal domestic demand stimulus, according to the ECB.

Disinflation is a dire consequence of interventionist policies, which lead to de-industrialisation and demand collapse.

Combating possible deflation risk with more interventionist policies while still curtailing the consumption capacity of citizens with higher taxes only leads us to enlarge the debt hole.

In addition, those calling for monetary stimulus forget that the velocity of money, which measures economic activity, collapses, creating a transfer of money to financial assets, stocks and bonds, and the collapse of productive investment. According to Citigroup, the velocity of money in the United States and the United Kingdom has fallen to levels last experienced in the mid-sixties, while nominal GDP is at 2001 levels. But the stock market is at historic highs and high-risk bonds at minimum yields. That is, we create "wealth illusion" in financial risk assets while sustaining GDP artificially but destroy wealth creation and employment.

We have to stop the vicious circle of spending, debt, impoverishment, financial repression, less wealth, less investment, higher unemployment and more spending and pass into a virtuous cycle of saving, budgetary restraint, improved disposable income, consumption, investment and employment.

Prosperity does not come from unicorn breeding, but consumption and productive investment.

Austerity is not pleasant. Austerity is painful. But bankruptcy hurts more than austerity, and it hurts more people for much longer.

PART III

HEDGE FUNDS AND THE STOCK MARKET

In the first section of this book, I wrote a very personal overview of the main elements that characterise the financial markets, their workings and investors' biggest concerns. In the second section, I went deeper into the current macroeconomic environment and the impact that government policies have had on developments in the stock market, fixed income and commodities during the last few years. I've also tried to explain the importance of solvency and liquidity equations for debt investors. I've done this by going over the most controversial elements of the recent economic crises, stimulus policies and possible solutions to what seems to be an increasingly uncertain economic environment.

For me, the crisis presents a great opportunity, challenge and chance to change past mistakes and the "bubble" mind-set; to redirect the habits and behaviour of all parties involved – from governments to small investors.

I will dedicate the third and final section of this book to explaining the workings of the world I have operated in – hedge funds. I'll tell you about my experiences, describe the investment process, give recommendations and highlight the tricks and mistakes investment managers make in their attempt to survive a complex but exciting environment.

I hope you enjoy this, and that it helps you in your personal investments, at least as another tool to go alongside your personal knowledge and common sense.

CHAPTER TWENTY-ONE

HEDGE FUNDS: THE BAD GUYS OF THE ECONOMIC CRISIS?

"The bank was always in debt." "It's a conspiracy among speculators." "The fundamentals are solid." "Everything is under control."

In these last years of the financial crisis, hedge fund managers have been the media's scapegoats, their favourite bad guys in articles, books, documentaries, films. I call this "blaming the waiter for the food in the restaurant". While the cooks and the owners of the establishments (central banks and governments) head down a suicidal path of monetary expansion (quantitative easing), low rates, debt and excess risk, the media finds its own Dr No in an abstract entity. A hedge fund has nothing to do with the media-created image of a bunch of cowboys pillaging markets and sinking countries. It is quite the opposite.

As soon as I started working in a hedge fund, I realised how much work I had in store for me. I went from analysing six to 150 companies. Days without a break until ten at night, Saturdays and Sundays too, spent not just following markets and their daily prices but analysing risks and portfolio composition. I had the lousy luck to catch a case of the measles.

Imagine it. I showed up in the United States full of hopes and plans of discovering the whole world, of learning everything I could, and by the second day I felt awful. I thought it was stress and nerves because of the new environment, so I went straight to my apartment at eight in the evening. When I woke up the following morning, my body looked like an oil exploration map. My co-workers at the investment fund laughed when they heard the news. "Nice first impression," they said.

I had to stay holed up in my apartment for a week. They had to leave my food at the door. In the good North American tradition of erring on the side of caution, I wore a surgical mask and gloves and they sent me in an ambulance to go to see the doctor, who was only two blocks from my apartment. They also contacted all the other passengers on the plane I came in on, to see if anyone else had caught the measles.

While I was in quarantine, I had the chance to use every second to get over the "decompression" process (as some colleagues called it). This is the period you need to stop being overwhelmed by the incredible amount of information that you take in every day, during which you learn to prioritise and manage stress. In a normal day, you receive around 2,500 emails and 120 buy or sell recommendations.

They'd also send me six reports an hour analysing whether my portfolio was in line with the risk limit variables and comparing it with the market, with my past performance, with the average of the other fund managers, with my expected performance and, most importantly, with indications of which percentile my performance fell within. The reason for this was to understand risk and that every quarter the portfolios of the worst performers would be reviewed.

At first, I didn't know how to handle all the information coming at me. There weren't enough hours in the day, and at night I dreamed about shares going up and down. Three of my co-workers left the firm because of this. Then suddenly one day it became clear. I can't tell you exactly how it happened, but it was basically a gradual process of getting rid of what wasn't relevant. Pressure helps you to learn to put aside the white noise of thousands of reports and to focus on the three or four aspects that really matter in the movement of a security, to only accept meetings with people who can add value and focus on monitoring the portfolio risk. Most of the public is unaware of the amount of risk analysis that is done as part of the daily operation of this type of investment fund. This is why, in my opinion, the media's demonisation of the industry is extremely misguided.

My son Pablo says that I "work all the time". This is another characteristic of the industry. No fixed working hours.

The image of hedge funds is distorted primarily for two reasons: first, because of the use of the so-called bearish positions (short positions), and, secondly, because of the incorrect perception that it is an industry made up of pirates where the managers make millions. It is a shame that the media spreads this image, because the big investors of these funds predicted the crisis and subprime mortgage and debt problems years ahead of time. They are then blamed for creating the crisis, when the only thing they did was show the world the reality and, of course, invest accordingly.

As for salaries, people don't understand that this industry only pays big bonuses when they are justified by profits. Managers put their reputation and money on the line along with their customers', as more than 75% of their bonuses are reinvested in their own funds.

By including short positions in their portfolio, a hedge fund provides the market with liquidity. A short position is an investment in an overvalued asset, which takes advantage of the backlash sustained until it reaches its correct fundamental value. What the public doesn't understand is that the short positions are only one element in the investment process.

Managers invest in securities and assets financed with short positions to mitigate for volatility in their portfolio, and thus have maximum risk control.

Without short positions, these funds can't take long (bullish) positions, and therefore many IPOs, capital increases, etc., would never come about without the participation of hedge funds. The investments are made with as much, if not more, financial and analytical rigour than in any investment bank. Keep in mind that this is a meritocracy based on results, and so it punishes and rewards.

"Alternative investment funds" are so called because their basic objective is to use the different instruments in the market to invest in the most rational way possible, while removing external influence and investment risk as far as possible from a particular asset.

The objective is to provide the investor with a team of experienced and prestigious professionals who have the capability and freedom to use all instruments available to actively take positions in the market, choose different maturation periods, borrow assets and use appropriate leverage to obtain high returns – without, of course, exposing the investor to unnecessary risk.

Hedge fund clients are not small minority shareholders or grandmothers buying from their bank's local branch. They tend to be high-net-worth individuals, pension funds and sovereign wealth funds. They are well aware of the number of current investments, liquidity, use, volatility and risk limits of the different products, be they derivatives, futures, indices, fixed or variable income securities, etc. Everything is detailed in the fund information.

To start with, the minimum amount for investing is usually about $500,000. As required by the FCA, SEC and other regulatory bodies, hedge fund clients must be qualified and sophisticated investors. Because of this, the brochures and subscription forms for these funds are extremely detailed.

It is precisely because there are imperfectly valued assets that can generate return for investors that the market represents an investment opportunity. This occurs as they move towards their real value relative to the industry, environment and country where they are listed. These imperfections do not always match rating expectations, and it is here that an alternative fund seeks to maximise profit. Opportunity can also be found in borrowing an undervalued (or correctly valued) asset with the objective of generating a return if the asset price falls, or providing liquidity to invest in a more attractive asset. Of course, in order to identify these opportunities, rigorous methods of analysis and estimation are used, as we will see later on.

CHAPTER TWENTY-TWO

ACTIVE MANAGEMENT

The supposed volatility and short-sightedness of financial markets that seem to concern governments and the press contrast with my experience and that of every other hedge fund manager I know. Their objective is simply to create a portfolio that grows in assets and minimises risk and transaction costs. All the critics seem to forget the significant commissions that are paid to buy and sell shares or exercise options: commissions that support the business of the investment banks and the depository institutions.

The manager seeks to create a portfolio that grows and generates returns in line with risk, with an investment horizon of between six and 12 months. The myth that hedge funds "buy and sell everything" in a day is just an exaggeration. In reality, the perfect portfolio would still contain at least more than half "good picks" after at least six months. It would be one upon which investments could be built and increased, without becoming a mix of too many instruments that were impossible to handle.

The manager of an optimal portfolio would have a maximum of 20% of the capital tied up in short-term ideas (those of less than three months) or picks defined by specific future events (a strategic presentation, an expected change in the management team, etc.). In short, it would be a portfolio that allowed its owner new opportunities to increase the invested capital and explore new ideas without aggressively having to buy and sell every day. In fact, most hedge fund managers consider very short-term operations (day trading) only as the final touch to a solid portfolio.

The manager seeks to generate alpha returns, or returns above beta (average-market performance), and for this reason may take short positions (asset loans) or long positions (traditional buys) in shares or commodities using arbitrages and negotiating options or bonds, and by investing in any opportunity where good returns are obtained with minor risks. Coverage against market trend changes is obtained by anticipating volatility and corrections, and taking advantage of the opportunities available (which can be long, medium or short term) through active management.

For a manager, an unexpected increase in the price of an asset can mean (depending on the case in hand) a chance to sell, an opportunity to go short or a chance to close a short position before taking the risk that it increases in value. In any case, active management gives liquidity to this asset, while offering additional opportunities to investors by reducing transaction costs in the meantime. As more operators buy and sell, the market becomes more competitive.

In general, the active management technique is based on technical analysis models (moving averages, volume indicators, etc.), combined with special models for each company, multiple comparison methods (P/E or price relative to earnings, EV/ EBITDA or enterprise value relative to earnings before taxes, depreciation and amortisation, PEG price to earnings growth, etc.) and absolute and relative price targets with buy and sell signals.

Let's look at an example. The table shows a particular sector of similar (industrial) companies and the EV/EBITDA multiple, which refers to the company's assigned value (market price plus debt) divided by its operating income before taxes, depreciation and amortisation, that is the best possible proxy to recurrent operating earnings. It is a common way of knowing how many times the asset price discounts company income. This multiple shows what price each company trades at now and in the past, and gives an estimate for the coming years.

	2011	2012	2013	2014E	Average 2011–2014
Stock A	7.0	9.6	6.6	5.4	7.1
Stock B	11.0	10.5	8.7	8.3	9.7
Stock C	6.3	6.7	5.8	5.4	6.1
Average EU	8.2	8.9	7.0	6.4	7.6
Average US	6.7	5.4	5.0	6.6	5.9
Overall average	7.5	7.1	6.0	6.5	6.8

Source: Company information, Bloomberg analysts' consensus

It is interesting to see that what seems to be a low price (low multiples) can be a "value trap" (securities that look cheap but traditionally have always been so). When this multiple has been reduced over time (in other words is increasingly assigned risk and low expectations), a clear risk is also reflected. It is also interesting to see that the "discount" some securities offer compared to similar organisations is structural, which is why something that seems undervalued often really isn't. These industries provide excellent short- and medium-term trades, and some investors may decide to make a United States versus Europe stock pairing (long versus short). Pure alpha.

There is no universal method of choosing. Rather, each manager uses their own techniques. For this reason, it is very important for the potential client to understand the difference between each manager's strategy and their track record. They are not all alike, and return on investment, volatility and risk vary substantially.

CHAPTER TWENTY-THREE

CRITICS AND REALITY

A strange thing about the controversy generated during these years is that it is precisely the process of opening "short positions" that has generated the most suspicion. Actually, the fact that an asset can generate an adequate return over time, be loaned out and therefore provide more liquidity and trading volume should be seen as something positive. Short positions are not "easy money", as the risk is asymmetric. A stock can go up by more than 100% but can never go down by more than 100%. Behind this criticism is a certain fear of the free-moving market and the possibility it holds over the impact of a particular news event, decision or strategic movement.

Why would the short interest (percentage of market capitalisation that is held in short positions) concern a company that was going to fulfil or exceed its targets, create value and defend its minority shareholders?

When I was working in the corporate world, I saw these situations as opportunities. If targets are reached, stock price increases more than expected when what is known as "short squeeze" is created. This happens when a large number of funds close their shorts (buy back the securities that they have loaned) following an event or positive surprise, providing a knock-on positive effect.

Another big concern is the (supposedly) high degree of leveraging with which an alternative management fund operates. Leveraging is the ratio between credit and the investor's own equity invested in a transaction or a portfolio; the degree of debt that comes into the strategy.

I believe that this is another myth. In my professional experience, leverage is completely correlated with the level of risk. In other words, given that funds operate with some very rigid risk parameters, the level of leverage is justified for low volatility. We also shouldn't forget that, unlike many traditional institutions, in this type of fund the manager shares the same returns and risks as the investor. And a hedge fund is not a suitable investment for uninformed shareholders. They charge management fees of about 1.75%, and minimum investment amounts are around $500,000. Every month, investors are informed in detail of the changes in the fund and their assets.

The apocalyptic vision of a group of cowboys moving the market at their whim quickly dissolves when the issue is examined more closely. In the (near 20,000) existing hedge funds, the large majority of the managers work under the most Darwinian and unequivocal pay systems in the world. Over 75% of salaries are tied to shares in the profits generated (by the manager, not by the fund). Furthermore, there is obvious personal risk, since it is common in the industry for portfolios to be reviewed quarterly or every six months. Therefore, managers have little interest in betting their prestige, career and salary on acting crazily. In fact, I've known few managers more conscientious in their analysis of companies and more detailed in their buying and selling process than hedge fund managers.

CHAPTER TWENTY-FOUR

STRATEGIES

From my point of view, one of the essential elements for separating the strategy of each hedge fund is to identify the level of risk/return trade-off sought. In fact, one of the mistakes that have been made in the last few years has been to look only at returns (16, 20 or 30%) and not returns based on assumed risk (VAR, or value at risk).

The VAR measures the percentage of invested money which can be lost in a portfolio, using a statistical simulation with a 95% confidence level (probability of getting it right) and different calculation methods. For example, if a security normally goes up or down by 1% daily, the VAR of the hypothetical portfolio made up only of this security is approximately 1%. The most common and simplest method of calculating VAR involves simulating the behaviour of the underlying risks of the asset through different scenarios. Risk factors are identified based on multiple regression models which include country risk, macroeconomic factors, commodity prices, interest rates, etc.

For every investment of $1 in a given asset, the percentage of this dollar that is being put "at risk" is estimated by considering what has occurred in the past.

Of course, the past does not necessarily identify everything that can make a trend rise or fall, but it is without doubt a very powerful tool because, although we often don't want to acknowledge it, the past tends to repeat itself and the securities market tends to have a sheep mentality. This is why technical analysis helps just as much as the analysis of fundamentals in the investment process: the behaviour of an asset is revealing. This analysis allows us to identify turning points that are also known as "resistances" (when maximums are being dealt with) and "supports" (when minimums are concerned).

For me the investment strategies most fitting of the term "alternative management" are those not correlated with general volatility, but rather ones able to turn out consistently high returns with extremely low loss risks. To build this kind of strategy, the manager must do a very detailed job of separating real opportunities from fictitious ones.

From my point of view, the process that has to be followed with each asset is divided into three parts: fundamental analysis, through estimation models and estimated future yield evaluation; identification of catalysts, or events that contribute to the asset's value when it confirms its performance expectations; and technical analysis.

Technical analysis according to Investopedia is a method of evaluating securities by analysing statistics generated by market activity, such as past prices and volume. Technical analysts do not attempt to measure a security's intrinsic value but instead use charts and other tools to identify patterns that can suggest future activity.

Using trends and pattern analysis, one can have a decent understanding of possible future performance.

I will now list some of the best-known investment strategies, and identify the standard leveraging levels based on volatility.

- Aggressive growth: Usually known as "multiples expansion" or "EPS-driven" growth. This involves investing in assets where it is believed that a trend is going to change, leading to an increase in earnings per share (EPS) that is higher than the historical average. This kind of strategy is normally accompanied by a very detailed study of the factors that "move" a share, and is usually oriented around a particular industry. Given the high volatility of the position and levels of risk that affect the prediction, leveraging is usually low.

- Arbitrage: This traditional "paired-trade strategy" (long/short) looks to compensate for external effects on securities following a given event (normally a merger or acquisition). It does so by taking positions in different assets of the same type, be they shares or futures. This is the strategy where the manager's value is most highly recognised. To the extent that the analysis of each asset is accurately reflected, a higher level of leveraging should be given.

- Sectorial: This involves investing long and short in a given sector with a management team made up of experts in this area. The return is entirely based on successful share picking. Given the low risk assumed, leveraging is usually high to cover most of the venture.

- Emerging markets: The favourite of many managers looking for a high short-term return, this is also a very risky strategy. If conditions are favourable, a share in an emerging country is usually subject to higher future growth than one in the same industry in other countries. However, it is also subject to higher risk, volatility and the threat of inflation. This increased risk is usually created owing to the difficulty of covering investment and of selling quickly if there is a crisis, although big securities are normally a lower-risk exception to this. This volatility and risk, in my opinion, can only be covered with another similar share in the same country and industry.

- Macro: In my point of view, a moderately risky strategy. This involves predicting global macroeconomic movements and their impact on the price of assets, interest rates, etc. It is significantly complex, and it can never be guaranteed that the identified trend will influence the price of assets in the time and manner expected. I believe this type of strategy must be sufficiently covered with low leveraging. I recall a colleague who made very complicated econometric models for investing that then were distorted by something as unpredictable as whether the hurricane season would hit the American coast.

- Special situations: Every fund has a definition of "special situation", but in general these are any investment that is out of reach via the normal buying and selling of financial instruments for an investor, e.g. funding a company before it is publicly traded, participating in capital increases for non-traded companies, investing in projects for the purpose of selling assets later or leveraging a share before selling it. The most complicated part is looking for the way to cover these investments. Normally, the best way is to cover them with a combination of futures and shares that counter the risk identified in this asset. Derivatives are usually used for increasing returns and compensating for risks, especially for interest rates in the case of funding. These are usually investments involving different professionals from the fund and, by their very nature, are treated very cautiously.

- Event-driven: This basically involves investing in assets on the basis of a very particular event or piece of news that is expected to have a dramatic impact on price. The objective is to draw alpha from this news, independently of the fundamental appeal or risks of the asset. This is a very complex activity, requiring a conscientious study of the situation and experience in order to identify points of inflexion and obtain positive returns regardless of the time that will pass before the event occurs (probably everybody will be thinking of the long takeover bid processes many large corporations go through and the changes in trading for these companies, depending on expectations). Initially, expected volatility should be low and is usually covered well with similar assets, which is why leveraging is often very high.

- Multiple strategies (multi-strat): Undoubtedly refer to what the large majority of the hedge funds do, i.e. diversify and reduce risk by using various strategies managed by professionals specialising in the industry at the same time. Each manager can improve their returns by incorporating different investment systems, by picking the right time to incorporate sector estimates and macroeconomics or by increasing exposure to long/short trading pairs as usually happens in uncertain situations.

CHAPTER TWENTY-FIVE

BUILDING PORTFOLIOS

In this chapter I'll focus on a special area of expertise, which is the management of a portfolio within the energy industry. If we do a brief review of the recommendations of the investment banks in early 2014, we will see that the oil industry, for example, seemed at first glance to be a great opportunity. The consensus of the target prices was between 25 and 35% higher than the current price, almost all recommendations were positive and the recommended companies were large and solid. Industry earnings between 2004 and the end of 2013 were greater than the S&P 500 (American exchange), but much lower than the increase in value of the greatest risk factor: the price of oil. Three factors can be identified that explain why these securities did not reflect the commodity that supposedly drove these profits: static multiples – companies that are too big, don't grow and trade for years at P/E 9-10x (ratio of share price to net profit) – consolidation (fundamentally as buyers) and negative macro factors like the increase in country risk when influence is lost in producer countries. It's important to know how to pinpoint, among other factors, when the industry will stay low-priced: the ROCE (return on capital employed) decreases and the cash flow generated decreases compared to the firm's value.

If we examine the utilities industry, we see that things are much worse than expected. This is especially true in Europe, where it has been, along with banks, the worst-performing sector on the stock market for nearly five years. Causes for this must be looked for in the destruction of value through high-priced strategic acquisitions, falling demand, some overly onerous investment plans, excessive debt and the threat of dividend cuts.

Both sectors pay good dividends (with yields of 5 to 6%) but oil pays with cash, while utilities tend to pay with debt or shares.

The logical thing in this environment is to try to create market-neutral portfolios using two supposedly closely correlated sectors which have significant strategic differences. It's important to keep a medium–long perspective (six, nine, 12 months) that is clearly oriented towards the fundamentals of each security. Using indices (FTSE, Dow, Ibex, CAC, DAX or sectorial) as a hedge is useful, but it is a good idea not to overuse indices, because in times of uncertainty this doesn't help maintain the generation of attractive returns.

In my experience, a manager can exhaustively monitor up to 150 companies by creating individual results analysis models, a simple profit and loss status, cash flow, the sum of the parts from each security and by using technical analysis, multiple regression models and share from inter-sector comparisons of multiples to identify opportunities for long and short investment.

It's strange that the most commonly heard phrase of analysts on the sell-side is "It's very hard to find shorts." This is due to the tendency to consider most pieces of news or events in terms of potential for increasing value, which is very logical when a limited number of companies are monitored in great detail. A bank analyst very rarely covers more than 10 companies.

It was also hard for me to identify shorts when I was an analyst. This was due to the tendency of analysts to see a strategic picture that is similar to that of the management team of the company, which is not necessarily a good horizon for investing unless they have infinite patience and the tolerance to lose money (or not earn any, which is the same if you consider opportunity cost and funding). Generally, the analysts' recommendations are usually 65% "buy" or "strong buy", 20% "stay" or "neutral" and 15% "sell". The interesting thing is that, in reality, there really are opportunities for opening lots of short positions, not necessarily in securities that are going to fall but in securities that perform worse than comparable ones.

Imagine that you invest in two securities listed on the same exchange which have similar fundamentals. Let's say two banks, one long and the other short. If the market rises and your long goes up by 10% and the short by 7%, the portfolio will have generated a profit of 3% with very little volatility and without exposure to external volatilities. This is called "alpha". If, on the other hand, the market falls by 5% because of macroeconomic or political rumours, your portfolio is well covered and it will not result in enormous losses to you.

Let's assume that you are wrong and invest "long" in the incorrect security, which goes up less and falls more than the other. You will then immediately know that your fundamental analysis of the relative strengths involved was wrong, and you will not be able to blame it on the market. Your decision as an investor created negative alpha. The job on the sell-side (brokers, banks) is essential for the manager, but it can't be forgotten that, ultimately, it's the manager who earns or loses money. Nothing justifies numbers in the red. The sell-side helps to identify different points of view, question the manager's ideas and recall otherwise bypassed opportunities to cover a greater spectrum of companies. In addition, the sell-side uses hedge funds to give contrast to their own estimates and detect buying and selling opportunities.

This is how a portfolio of very competitive securities can be built with a relatively stable core of big long-term position investments comprising some seven to 10 securities. Between six and eight long-short positions will be added to this core, which should generate short-term opportunities on the basis of monitoring quarterly returns and events including identifiable macroeconomic movements like the price of oil owing to geopolitical crisis, declines from excess supply or the debt environment in the oil-producing countries. (A long-short is the combination of positions expected to outperform or go up [longs] and the ones expected to underperform or go down [shorts].)

Portfolio vs. index

Once we have built a neutral portfolio, we will then analyse the risk elements to which the portfolio is exposed in a given month. To do this, we would use multiple regressions which allow the manager, at any time, to revise levels of return, risk, sensitivity, exposure to risk factors, as well as profit-taking opportunities and volatility exposure for each stock or asset-class that might have recently moved in an unusual way.

Of course, in the end, building a portfolio is a personal and individual process, and there are no magic formulas. However, something I have learnt over time is that detailed analysis and fundamental knowledge of the companies and their management teams in question is essential. In a changing environment, sometimes you're right and sometimes you're wrong. But to create a portfolio where at least 56% of the ideas generate greater returns than the market, there is something that usually works: "the fundamentals prevail".

CHAPTER TWENTY-SIX

CLOSENESS MAKES THE HEART GROW FONDER: HOW TO IDENTIFY INVESTMENT OPPORTUNITIES

What do you do at the weekend? Most of the time, managers are doing deep analysis: reading and rereading company analyses and going over possible buy and sell opportunities, what worked and what didn't. On Friday, teams prepare a portfolio assessment that is reviewed over the weekend. It is made up of the following elements:

- Reinvestment signs: Go over those securities that have had an exceptional performance, whether positive or negative, and look at the possible signs of strength or weakness compared to similar securities. This allows analysts to anticipate, to the greatest extent possible, the so-called dead cat bounce of securities with poor fundamentals. However, these may rise, often gathering profits and later increasing short positions.
- Stop-loss, take-profit: Review securities to collect profits and cut losses. It is very important to know how to recognise when we have made mistakes and cut our losses. Don't hold onto a wrong idea or look for justifications to dig into a deeper hole; don't wait for a miracle. When positions are

taken and the market shows us that they are wrong, let go of these operations before they eat up the profits of the other securities.

- Ideas to consider: The team presents their best ideas to include in the portfolio. This involves deciding what can go in and what cannot, and above all what should come out so that a new security can go in.
- Global trends and exposure: We analyse the risk factors to which we are consciously or unconsciously exposed.

Funds normally do an analysis of pricing anomalies of securities with respect to the industries they are found in at a global and local level, regardless of whether they are over- or under-valued. It is important also to analyse the catalysts for each security, in other words which news events would adjust this valuation to what is considered the correct one. Funds also hold meetings with the companies involved. Lastly, analyse external, regulatory, legal and governmental factors, and their possible impacts on the price of the share.

Teams of analysts look for expensive securities to open short positions and attractive securities to open long positions. Their work is monitored week by week and month by month. It is also very useful to talk to other investors, especially those who have not been investing. A lot is learnt by speaking to investors who prefer to stay "liquid" and not participate in the market, regardless of whether they are bullish or bearish.

Of course, funds also develop a direct analysis of every company. Essential evaluation tools include ROCE, cost of capital, working capital and cash flow and global and regional macroeconomic analyses. When this type of analysis is performed, it has to be kept in mind not only that the market is inefficient but also that it tends to be optimistic.

One of the areas of focus is analysing sectors during the process of losing value or "de-rating". This means investigating, for example, sectors that are listed at a P/E 14, but will list at P/E 8 in two years owing to the erosion of profits and the increase in working capital. Clear cases were renewable energy in 2007, construction in 2008, telecoms in 2009 and the big oil companies between 2005 and 2010 or gold miners in 2012–2013.

It is also very important to analyse whether the estimates of returns are over- or undervalued. There is nothing like scrutinising securities in search of profit warnings (downward revisions to companies' forecasts). In 2012, many funds detected indicators of this type in nearly 33% of large companies. Obviously, this same process goes also with companies that exceeded their forecasts. There are big opportunities for upward and downward corrections based on fundamentals. Supposedly inexpensive companies stay just as low-priced after a 50% fall because profits fall, and supposedly expensive companies are marked down cheaper despite going up 20% because earnings were better than estimated.

Investment process

There is something essential that must be understood about a hedge fund: each manager is entirely responsible for their portfolio. There may be several managers of different portfolios, whose collective sum makes up a fund, but every manager takes responsibility for their own portfolio. The fundamental analysts help complement them by making forecasts for the companies that come into the investment universe, and the risk analysts review the exposure limits to given factors. But in the end the decision comes down to a single person: the manager.

It is precisely the combination of clear risk limits and maximum market exposure that dismantles the theory of hedge funds as huge machines that generate enormous volatility as they enter and exit the stock market. In fact, volatility control is much more exhaustive than in traditional funds. Alternative funds usually have volatility of less than 14%, while volatility in traditional funds approaches 25%. Teams use quantitative analysis to create investment recommendations. These investment recommendations must be clear, concise and short: three sentences. There is no security or investment in the world that cannot be summarised in three sentences. For example, the three sentences could be: "Trades at a 20% discount over comparable companies in EV/EBITDA, but profit generation is changing and in a year it will generate the same ROCE as the rest. Over the next three quarters, we will see a debt reduction of 20% and a 15% improvement in earnings. Pay attention to the strategic presentation that they will make mid-year to confirm their dividend increase." These three sentences pinpoint where the company is at this time, where we think it is going to be in the future and what information corroborates or invalidates our thesis. If it turns out to be wrong and the security begins to fall, it's important to revise the investment idea and sell. It is essential to be concise and clear about the reasons for buying or selling an asset and to put it in writing, so as not to fool ourselves. One of the biggest mistakes that we sometimes make as investors is to buy something because it has high growth and spectacular earnings, and then to classify it as a "long-term position" after this proves wrong.

There is more than one way to skin a cat, but in many cases teams use quantitative analysis with various combinations of multiples to see whether an asset is suitable for buying or selling. Funds develop our internal models from a starting point of information from analysts, banks, consultants and companies. They are based on our perspective on future variables and our knowledge of companies and governments. And the question is always "How much can we lose?", not just "How much can we earn?"

This process leads us to reject securities every day if they do not meet the requirements for growth, margins and company management involvement. To the maximum extent possible, it is essential to keep interests in line with those of the executive management directors. When the managers of the companies earn a lot and own few shares, alarms go off. Of course, a lot of the securities rejected as attractive for a long position go to the list of candidates for short positions. There are no "hold" or "no recommendation" securities in a hedge fund. They are either sold or bought.

Think of companies as financial securities, not as industrial enterprises.

It is important to distinguish between "shares" as financial assets and the company as an industrial asset, because many people mistakenly identify a "good company" as a "good security" and in many cases this is not true. Good companies can be bad investments, as we have seen in so many large conglomerates. I always say that one thing is to think of a company as a place to send your CV to, and another to look at it as a stock, as an investment. This is why you may use in a portfolio the same stock as a long and afterwards as a short or vice versa over the course of one or two years. This is not a marriage; it is an investment.

As I noted earlier, a lot can also be learnt from investors who decide not to participate in the market at a given time and hold cash. Perhaps because they believe that the environment is overly upbeat or have expectations of returns that are impossible to achieve. These are often people who pay attention to balance and credit sheets as they should, as opposed to those who always say that "Everything is undervalued" or "If you set this security at historical multiples, it has a 30% increase" and so forth. I recall a friend from an institutional fund (long only) who used to say: "If I could open short positions, I would do it now." His comment helped me revisit my thoughts. Investors outside this realm are not trying to sell you securities that they already have, and they don't try to justify their invested position.

There are those who say that 50% of short-term share movements (appreciation or depreciation) can be explained by the overall developments in the market (beta), another 30% are explained by developments in the sector and only 20% by developments in the company itself. This is a big myth. Take the three- to five-year changes in the oil industry, for example, which are supposedly highly correlated with and influenced by underlying commodities. You will see that the performance (spread of returns) among the securities, including the heavy-weights of the index, is between 15 and 20%.

The fundamentals matter much more than passive and indexed investors usually care to acknowledge. Up to 56% of the performance of a security can be intrinsic; as far as the remainder, it's true that the market matters a bit more than the sector.

CHAPTER TWENTY-SEVEN

SHORT POSITIONS IN A PORTFOLIO

Why do I have shorts? For the summer.

Trader's comment

As I mentioned previously, "short" investing is the process whereby an investor borrows a security in exchange for interest payments and immediately sells it in order to repurchase it later at a, preferably, lower price than initially. They then return the loan with a profit. What is often not understood is that a short doesn't always have to be a bearish position as the press says. In most cases, it is a way of funding an investment in another security that is considered to have greater bullish potential. It is part of what is known as "long-short". So, when we short sell, we are basically looking to mitigate the risk that we take in another security that we consider more attractive. The process of short selling creates three benefits for the market: it increases liquidity for securities, allows a security to react more solidly to news or an event by broadening the buy/sell reaction and therefore gives companies that are telling us that the market is wrong a chance to prove they're right. For their part, the lender of the security not only receives interest but also sees its liquidity improve should they want to sell or buy more.

In most cases, the person taking a short position has done an analysis of the sector, the company and its competitors, and has seen that this security is a good funding source for another investment. For this reason, they pay interest on the borrowed security. The investor sees that the total cost of this position, including interest, mitigates the risk of their "long" positions. It can also generate a profit if, in addition to doing worse than its sector, it falls in absolute terms (because its results are poor or it destroys value). Of course, the manager can be mistaken. When this happens, the shorts are covered at a higher price and the management team can feel proud of having beaten the market. As it should be.

Let's imagine that a majority shareholder of a company with problems and poor fundamentals has made the decision to increase their position to 30%, from the share of more or less 15% that they currently hold. When other investors are increasing their short positions, how can this be explained?

What the majority shareholder is doing is called "stake building": the practice of increasing significant shareholding to a level that does not require making a public offering of shares or taking control. This is a transparent, legal and widespread activity. The majority shareholder can increase their participation in this "troubled company" for various reasons. After a sharp fall, value can be assumed to be cheap. Or perhaps the shareholder wants to increase their financial share in a security that they know well, where they can reduce the entry price by buying very low (this is known as "doubling down"). In addition, it could be that they know something that the rest do not, which allows them to presume that the price is going to greatly increase (this is much more difficult because it requires privileged information).

On the other hand, some investors may increase their short positions because they assume that it is not the time to buy, and that when this period is over substantial depreciation of the security will be generated. There are big firms that specialise in short positions for companies with fundamental problems where a stake-building process is occurring. We saw this in Europe in 2006 to 2007, for example, when companies built defensive positions in energy companies, banks bought stakes and so on. Defensive strategies are often a sign of weakness. Many funds took short positions, and generated significant profits.

They also may not care what the majority stakeholder does, and simply estimate that changes in price will be worse compared to those of similar competitors in the United States or the EU. Lastly, they may assume that the majority shareholder's purchase is merely defensive and designed to increase obstacles to splitting up or selling the company ("poison pills") by making the security even less attractive.

Who is right? Perhaps no one. These are two distinct investment strategies, both acceptable and both with different maturation periods. In any case, the best advice for the private investor is never to invest during the enthusiasm of "fund flows", which we investors call "piggy-backing": buying because someone else is buying or selling because someone else is short selling. We are never fully certain of which process led to choosing these investments, and we have seen too many big investors make mistakes with big long or short positions to copy or rate their investment decision. You should only ever buy based on your personal opinion of the fundamentals of a stock.

The job of the company, like that of all securities with a high percentage of shorts, is to obtain good returns, exceed forecasts, show that they can improve margins compared to their competitors and not blame external monsters. If they are mistaken, let them be mistaken. It will be reflected in their stock sooner or later. That's the beauty of the market.

CHAPTER TWENTY-EIGHT

BANNING SHORT SELLING AND THE TOBIN TAX

There were big drops in the stock market in August of 2011, which led to a new wave of intervention like we saw in 2008. Short selling was banned in many European countries. When the stock markets crash, governments (used to thinking that everything must always go up and that no drop is ever justified) believed that an intervention was necessary. The first thing that they usually do is blame short positions. However, according to Merrill Lynch and Goldman Sachs, more than $40 billion in shares was sold in the big 2011 crash, and $30.5 billion of these did not come from evil speculators or automated robotic systems, but from pension funds and institutions: the so-called long-only long-term investors. They were selling in the face of the excessive risk they saw in company returns and an economic environment that was rapidly deteriorating.

In 2012, short positions were once again banned for several months. We were repeating the mistakes of 2008 because, after the bans, trading volumes and trade in securities fell and volatility increased. If the economy's fundamentals are not solid, intervention will not keep the markets from falling. Since selling (naturally) cannot be banned, other means must be looked for to provide calm, means that actually create greater concern.

The constant interventions against capital flows that were applauded in 2012 included means like limiting company voting rights, introducing confiscatory taxes and Spain's decision to be the only country in the OECD to ban short selling.

With all short selling banned, the Spanish stock market performed in a similar way to the Portuguese and Italian stock markets, which did not have the ban and were just as European, indebted and peripheral as the Spanish market. Nevertheless, trading volumes crashed. A success. A 36% decline in volume and 40% in transactions.[18]

Banning short selling is a failure to understand how the market works. If it is perceived that there is intervention and manipulation in a stock market, investing simply stops. This is why trading volumes suddenly fell. In 2008, the stock market that rose the most was Zimbabwe's. No manager's bonus was reduced or criticised for "not being invested" in a manipulated stock market.

There are a lot of myths going around about short selling. For example, that it is a new financial engineering tool, when actually it has existed since 1949. Another myth is to think that short positions "sink" share prices. Share prices fall when returns and the financial situation worsen. Why didn't short positions affect good stocks that were just as peripheral in Europe as any other in 2012? Because their returns were improving faster. However, the biggest mistake, as I was saying in the previous chapter, is to call them "bearish" positions, because most of them are in fact used to finance long positions.

The decision to ban short positions denotes weakness and instils a lack of confidence. When this stays in place for a long

---

[18] Bolsas y Mercados Españoles.

time, it results in openly negative effects. Banning shorts actually multiplies volatility, curtails volumes and increases trading costs. With such low volumes and poor liquidity, both dips and swells are exaggerated. Any investor with more than 200 million under management simply cannot take on a dry, controlled and ultra-volatile market. The Spanish Stock Market Commission made clear in its 2011 report that "it is difficult to refute the positive effects that short sales have on liquidity, efficiency and even in the stability of stock markets".

The 2008 ban on short sales did not have any bullish effect on securities subject to intervention, and did not make the securities perform better than the Italian, Greek or Portuguese securities that did not have restrictions.

The fear of short selling has never been founded on facts, just on the myth that foreign investors can affect fundamentals. Or that long-term investors don't panic. Neither is correct.

CHAPTER TWENTY-NINE

RECOMMENDATIONS

Be careful with the famous "book value" for analysing a share, because in many cases it is a mirage. Many of the assets classified within these book values are bought at very high prices and with debt. These types of ratios, often repeated to justify buy recommendations, take excessive debt as an irrelevant anomaly. But if my asset is worth 10 and I incurred a debt of 100 units when buying it, my book value is irrelevant and the value of my asset may be exactly zero.

Funds use various dynamic evaluation methods (for a future reach of one, two and three years):

- The first is the EV/IC/ROIC/WACC (enterprise value compared with invested capital, returns and the cost of capital), which measures what I pay today for value creation of the investment process.
- Another is the FCF (free cash flow) yield and combined multiples of P/E (price earnings ratio), PEG (price/earnings to growth), EV/EBITDA (enterprise value compared with

earnings before interest, tax, depreciation and amortisation). These are always adjusted for debt and of course always look to the relative, rather than individual, value in each sector.

Other things to be aware of are:

- Be careful about getting carried away by future growth that is already more than paid for in present value.
- Remember that earnings per dividend are a misleading indicator. First, because many of these dividends are calculated as a percentage of net earnings. In other words, if net earnings are inflated, so are dividends. Second, because if the return on a 10-year Spanish bond is, for example, 5.3%, the average earnings for Ibex dividends, 5.8%, is not enough to compensate for the market risk. Going with dividends in an inflationary environment if the cash flow generated doesn't cover the amount allocated is dangerous, because the risk premium rises.
- It is a good idea to be careful about exposure to emerging markets if we don't understand the value creation proposition. The excuse that these developing countries offer high-percentage profits usually doesn't hold: first of all, because in many cases these profits have been acquired at a high price and, second, because the profits in emerging markets also have capital costs and their own market risks. For example, all the Inditex external growth is organic, while that of the banks and telecommunications is purchased. This has an influence on the multiples that the security is traded at.
- Keep an eye on the debt environment. This especially goes for the risk of default of small and medium-sized European companies in the next five years: low-priced, but debt-burdened, securities may suffer if there is another credit squeeze.

What is happening, as always, is that we have forgotten the true fundamentals: return on capital employed. There is no long-term strategy that cannot be monitored and is not perfectly measurable on a quarterly basis. And in many cases, long-term reasoning blinds us to how difficult it is going to be to reach these consensus estimates in view of the quarterly results.

Russell Napier said that the value of a share is "the glimmer of hope that exists between the assets and the liabilities of a company". We had forgotten the enormous weight of debt despite practically 0% interest rates, and the fragility of the returns generated by these assets. It is very hard to tell the big executives of European conglomerates this, but when less ROCE is generated with more capital expenditures (investments, organic or not), the asset becomes more expensive even when its price goes down.

In my opinion, there are basically two lessons to be learnt from the stock-market panic. The first is not to look for safety or stability in the securities of the indices, because this doesn't work. When the big institutional funds "long only" sell, the axe inevitably falls on the big companies. The second is that we should not lose sight of the fundamentals. After a bloodbath, there are still low-priced and expensive securities despite the drop, in the same way that lesser-priced securities still exist despite a steep rise. Closely measure the differential between the ROCE and the cost of capital (WACC) for each dollar spent in these grand manoeuvres of growth from investments and acquisitions, because it is what has the most influence on the shares' performance. Avoid the very dangerous "consensus longs" (securities that come highly recommended by invest-ment houses and that everyone has in their portfolio), avoid "cheap" securities that have always been inexpensive ("cheap for a reason") and basically avoid buying securities today based on past glories.

I always say that the best way to pick a good short position or a sell when you are reading stock market analysis or reports is when you find phrases like "It's a good company", "The fundamentals haven't changed" and "The dividend is attractive", because they are talking about the past, about vague or irrelevant elements. Here's why:

- "It's a good company" turns out to be irrelevant when it comes to generating higher returns in the future, which is what you are buying in a share. Remember to distinguish between industrial company and financial worth.
- "The fundamentals haven't changed" usually means that the company lives off income from a glorious past, and the returns will be poor in the upcoming quarters.
- "It has a good dividend yield" usually hides low growth, very mature businesses and declining returns. The dividend is deducted entirely from the price of the share and often it is paid with debt or, worse, with shares.

It is very dangerous to invest in "safe havens" with apparently high dividends or with a zero or negative change in earnings per share (EPS), because we are in an inflationary environment where interest rates cannot rise as higher rates could destroy the fragile OECD economy. Inflation added to low interest rates and tax hike risks is not a good formula for buying defensive sectors.

Investing in dividends if the free cash generation doesn't cover this dividend is dangerous, because it eats up the financial resources of the company and weakens it. The reasoning that a high percentage of profits is coming from emerging markets, as we have said, doesn't reduce the risk of a conglomerate discount, which is the most important issue in many of these cases, and increases the cost of capital (WACC).

The securities that did the worst from 2008 to 2013 were victims of downward revisions of earnings forecasts, not just portfolio turnover or "macro" issues.

Invest in securities with a good combination of growth, a low debt burden, cost controls, free cash flow and high ROCE in the downside of the business cycle. Whether they are defensive or not. But don't choose securities just on the basis that they have done relatively badly. Securities that look cheap can be very expensive for your wallet.

Watch out for consensus and crowded trades

Financial behaviour theory suggests that the markets are moved by two factors: greed and fear. I recommend that you read *Beyond Greed & Fear* by Hersh Shefrin. In my opinion, whatever the market sentiment, what you have to watch out for is finding yourself excessively positioned in "consensus" or "crowded trade" securities – those securities that practically everyone considers attractive and are highly recommended by investment banks. These are sometimes called "grandma stock" because even your grandmother knows about it.

The biggest risks in a market, whether it's bullish or bearish, are "consensus buy" securities. When the market falls, these securities are subject to the same selling pressure as others. When it rises, on the other hand, they rise equally or less than the indices, owing to being overly represented in most portfolios. By contrast, during an upward swing, the securities that rise the most are the less "consensual" securities, those where short positions occupy a greater percentage of the capital.

Unless you decide to work at identifying floors in the market (the riskiest investment strategy), the biggest risk is "turning into consensus": participating in the falls in all their glory, but never seeing tuppence from the upturns.

But where is the consensus?

Let me identify some warning signs:

- If you have invested in "safe" positions in big conglomerates, with decent dividends, exposure to emerging markets and "high-but-manageable" debt in cyclical sectors (industrials, automotive and oil), you run the risk of being "consensus". If you have gone into sectors that are very cyclical but hit hard in the market (solar-renewable energy, consumption), there is also a "consensus" risk.
- Even worse, if you have bought, supposedly, defensive securities that were cheap after several quarters of poor returns, you are invested in a "value trap": low-priced securities whose prices will stay low. If you identify "cheap" securities in a country that has European, American or sector equivalents that are also "cheap", it is very difficult for them to rise above the average of their competitors. It seems obvious, but I keep hearing people talk about how cheap this or that company is on its own merits, or even worse, compared to an index with which it has no relationship with regard to earnings, even if it trades at 10 to 12% above its sector.

When a "consensus" security does not end up rising, the worst possible effect is created, since investors, tired of putting up with "value traps", sell even if they do so at a loss. Nevertheless, it is worth looking out for these "cheap for a reason" securities, because they are the best ones for creating a portfolio of long-term short positions.

Beware following government messages

I have a good friend and reader who sometimes tells me: "This is going up: it's all very well controlled." Nevertheless, we forget that politicians and central banks are reactive entities. In other words, they usually get there too late. Unless you are an expert in technical analysis and predicting inflections and trend changes, the "invest because some politician says this or that" policy is what we call the "widow maker". With some luck it works once, but over the span of a year you get burnt time and time again.

Many times, politician comments are a good indicator to "sell when it's up" more than "buy when it's down". However, the mentality of the average investor tends to see bearish movements as "anomalies" and bullish movements as confirmation of worth. It's strange, but in investor psychology the "fear and greed" stimuli tend to lead us to buy and not to sell.

According to various American studies, the vast majority of investor losses don't result from inaccurate fundamental analysis, but from keeping securities "a little bit longer" when they have worked well.

The true fundamentals (earnings and margins, cash and the bottom line) are what count. In the vast majority of cases, over the span of a year, stock market changes are not the fault of Merkel or Yellen but are more or less directly reflected in the ups and downs of the expected profits. Between 2007 and 2013, most of the market indices we follow moved in almost perfect correlation to the downward or upward revision of consensus.

Pay attention to the cost of capital

Many companies use a combination of debt and equity to finance their businesses, and their overall cost of capital is derived from a weighted average of all capital sources, widely known as the "weighted average cost of capital" (WACC). Since the cost of capital represents a hurdle rate that a company must overcome before it can generate value, it is extensively used in the capital budgeting process to determine whether the company should proceed with a project.

The average weighted cost of capital together with ROCE (return on capital employed) are the most important metrics for the valuation of a stock. However, we pay very little attention to these metrics, because they are not attractive or easy to calculate, just like we don't pay attention to working capital and cash flow or focus on the profit and loss account that represents a financial year. And we tend to undervalue the equity risk premium of a security. As I previously mentioned, when they say that a security is very well supported by its dividend yield they often forget that this dividend yield is, on one hand, less than the risk premium liability of the security and, on the other, less than the sovereign debt coupon.

In 2011, I did a survey among investments banks that we worked with. The question was: "How much have you revised the equity risk premium upward on securities to discount their cash flows?" Answer: zero. Nothing. While countries' risk premiums were shooting through the roof, the "credit crunch" risk was becoming obvious and expected earnings revisions continued to fall, the adjustment to the average cost of capital was nil.

Let's say the price of a share is the sum of its future cash flows divided by the cost of capital. If the numerator goes down (cash flows are revised downwards) and the divisor goes up (the cost of capital), what happens to the price of the share? It falls.

I found myself in the same situation in 2012, when the risk premiums were going down and the central banks launched new stimulus programmes: nobody was revising the cost of capital downwards. It is not surprising that, in the face of these injections of liquidity and lowering sovereign risk, the most debt-burdened securities were the ones that had the best stock market performance. In fact, their earnings (cash flows) were not improving, but the impact of the cost of capital on their valuation was much more substantial.

Of course, it is not easy to anticipate abrupt movements of the cost of capital like those I have mentioned. However, it is at least worth understanding their impact on the securities in which we invest in order not to suffer losses and be told that "it's already discounted". Analysing upward or downward revisions to consensus forecasts and paying attention to the cost of capital seem to me to be essential exercises that explain a lot more than that well-worn phrase: "the speculators are attacking".

In a bear market the investor is never conservative enough

One of the biggest mistakes that all of us make as investors, of which I am as guilty as anyone, is to assume that our investment decision is very conservative. We also consider negative factors to be "noise" or "anomalies". If there is something that still surprises me every day, it's that we ignore external risk factors (country, currency, sectorial, credit risks) as "non-fundamental".

I think that it is important to summarise some of the points I've brought up, because both companies and investors almost constantly make the following mistakes:

- Omitting or ignoring the macroeconomic environment. The famous reasoning of "focusing on the fundamentals", when there is nothing that has more of an impact on the cost of capital than changes in the macroeconomic indicators. The cost of capital, as I mentioned previously, is one of the most important elements for evaluating a share.
- Ignoring strategic flows and the multiples at which comparable assets trade at a global level. Local companies and investors usually watch the trading of their shares as if the rest of the world didn't exist, without analysing why competitors lose or gain value. One of the biggest mistakes is to study how multiples change in the trading of security while continuing to focus on absolute price.
- Obsessing over buy recommendations. Although there are exceptions, most stock market recommendations tend to be

positive or neutral and, therefore, have less influence and standing among investors. Amassing large amounts of buy recommendations in a security doesn't mean anything in the medium term.

- Ignoring a rise in the correlation between securities and sectors. Globalisation and immediate access to information give securities greater and greater correlation (their changes in the stock market are very similar).

Be careful of dividends

Buying shares with good dividends is one of the most typical market strategies. It is perfectly legitimate and offers good results when you pay attention to the quality of these dividends, but you should not undervalue the risk that they will be cut.

Betting on big dividends of debt-ridden stocks with decent but decreasing earnings is a risky bet, as it ignores the risk of seeing such dividends cut, especially in a risk-averse period amidst banks' recapitalisation and global deleveraging. In the best-case scenario, this will increase the cost of debt. In the worst case, it will reduce available credit even further. On the other hand, in an uncertain growth environment it is essential to reconsider companies' optimum debt. American companies, for example, have been doing this since 2007 because they were afraid of the new administration, while in Europe debt by sector has continued to be much higher than average because many companies choose to stay "excellently positioned for the return of growth".

When you choose securities by their dividends, you should understand where this dividend comes from and how it is paid for:

- When dividends paid exceed the surplus amount from the margins of ordinary activities, they are discounted by more than 100%. In other words, the share cuts the dividend coupon and is an additional element of value destruction.

- Many of these dividends are paid with debt.
- A large part of these dividends come from "purchased" earnings, through acquisitions that destroy value (84% of acquisitions since 1996 have generated negative added value), with which they have done nothing to revalue the share. Someone can pay whatever dividend they want, but this doesn't compensate for the destruction of value.

On the plus side:

- Dividends are paid for by companies that generate cash which more than covers their investments and have healthy balance sheets. Not only are they stable and can provide nice surprises (being revised upwards) but they also add value for the shareholder without putting the soundness of the company in danger.
- Paying a "special" dividend when a sale of assets is made that generates a good accounting sheet profit (its sale price is higher than it was valued in the company books) is a wise practice, since it compensates the shareholder and avoids the temptation to spend on poor investments.

CHAPTER THIRTY

THE LONG-TERM ILLUSION... AND THE OPPORTUNITY OF VALUE INVESTING

One of the media's favourite sayings is: "The market is very short-sighted." What happens is that the market is wary and has more than enough reason to be.

Not only do forecasts matter for a stock, confidence is also an important factor driving the "discount factor". This is because the investor purchases a share, which at the end of the day is the present value of future earnings, the discounted free cash flows of a company. We forget that as the debt increases the risk premium also increases, no matter how low the cost of the debt.

However, it's worth doing a more careful analysis of the reasons why the market is wary. For investing "long term", let's say five years, we basically have to assume the following:

- The macroeconomic forecasts of the countries where the security generates its earnings are sustainable.
- A moderate element of inflation exists, which justifies the value of the replacement of the company's share (the sum of the parts).

- The strategic plans will not only be fulfilled, but the planned investments will create value (a return higher than the cost of capital) within an acceptable maturation period of about three years.

After the first two reasons for investing have been established, the surprise comes, especially in that third element. As we've mentioned, companies tend to undervalue their cost of capital. Worse still, many companies often behave pro-cyclically (buy when everything is going up, and sell when everything is going down), because in expansionary times they fall prey to the temptation to "improve" their capital cost by increasing debt, while at the same time they should consider that the risk premium is also increasing.

Sound companies with good balance sheets embark on "strategic" ventures. According to information from the big banks, more than 75% of the mergers and acquisitions between 1990 and 2012 destroyed value for shareholders of the purchasing company.

There is an additional problem. The mean career of a CEO of a company has been reduced by 21% in the last ten years. How can we invest in the long term when a management team changes every six years on average? The companies' strategic plans are usually five years, but according to Thomson Reuters more than 65% of these plans are not fulfilled or are revised.

A professional investor is not paid for putting up with a share that destroys value in the short term, or for overestimating valuations. Even the most basic fund watches how its clients monitor monthly earnings. The investor must calibrate precisely the risk return that it takes on for a long-term investment, and avoid optimistic projections. Today, investors cannot easily trust that valuations will be attractive for more than two years when you consider how quickly risk perception moves.

Thanks to the Internet and specialised media, the investor has an enormous amount of information at hand to make correct decisions but should be aware of increases in a security's volatility and risk premium owing to macroeconomic changes. However, long-term investments can be made as long as some essential elements are taken into account, which I will talk about with the collaboration of two experts in the field in the following section.

Value investing: All is well that starts well

All my scepticism towards what many investors call "the long term" comes from the fact that the phrase is often used as an excuse for past losses. However, a good analysis can provide us with great investment opportunities. The "value investing" that Warren Buffett made fashionable is much more complex than minority shareholders think. My good friend Pablo J. Vázquez helped me to differentiate between "value investing" and a "value trap".

It is impossible to describe in a single chapter the steps you should follow before saying "yes, I want this" to a given security. Nevertheless, I will try to show you what I think are the key elements of this decision, and describe my current way of understanding the markets. I would highlight the following:

Good liquidity

When I talk about liquidity, I am not referring to company shares that can be easily sold without taking on a significant discount. I am talking about a financial situation: can the company take on the payment of all of its short-term debt?

Experience tells me that when a company shows some weakness in this sense, the market will not take long in penalising it. The "current ratio" or "quick ratio" can be used to help us determine the company's short-term payment capacity. This is an accounting ratio that measures a company's ability to pay its current liabilities with its current assets (current assets divided by current liabilities). If the current ratio is less than one, this indicates a situation where there is a risk.

Low leverage

To put it briefly: little debt. The property bubble that has been so intensely experienced in Spain is a clear reflection of the dangers of massive leveraging. Layers and layers of debt did nothing but mask a reality that later became obvious. Excessive debt is usually the tip of the iceberg of bad companies.

The debt to capital ratio provides us with a very clear snapshot of a company's degree of leveraging. Imagine that the purchase of all the assets held by a company has been financed either with borrowed funds (liabilities) or with their own (net worth). The debt ratio is nothing more than the quotient between these two magnitudes. If this quotient is greater than one, it means that the volume of debt is more than the capital contributed by the shareholders.

High gross margins

We can distinguish between two types of cost in a company: on one side, those costs that are directly related to the manufacturing of a product or rendering of a service; on the other, those costs that only come into play indirectly. For example, in the first section, we could include the labour costs for those who operate a given machine or the cost of the purchased raw goods; in the second, we could include, for example, the payments to administrative personnel or advertising costs. For defining the gross margin, what interests me are direct costs, more commonly known as "sales costs".

So, the gross margin is defined as the difference between sales revenue and the cost of these sales per unit sold. That is:

$$\text{Gross margin} = \frac{\text{Sales} - \text{Cost}}{\text{Total sales}}$$

Excellence is usually guaranteed by a high gross margin. And it's not just me saying it; two of the most acknowledged investors in the world also say so: Warren Buffett and Ken Fisher.

A profitable business

Profitability. This is the pillar of all investment strategies. If this fails, nothing else matters. In fact, I can accept a company strategy that may contain some flaws as long as profitability is achieved and maintained.

First, the concept. If you lend me money and I give it back to you after a year along with another €1,000, would you take the deal? The answer is obvious: it depends on the amount you lent me. Receiving €1,000 in interest on a €10,000 loan (10% profit) is not the same as receiving €1,000 for a €100,000 loan (1% profit).

What you are really concerned with here is the profitability of invested capital, to put it another way the profit per unit invested. It is the same with a company. A given profit will be good or bad depending on the amount of capital invested to obtain it.

Here, we need to follow a recipe. There are different ways of understanding profitability, but I am very clear about mine: I want to know how profitable the assets are that are used in the operating activity of the company. I need two ingredients: on one side, the operating profit, also known as earnings before interest and taxes (EBIT), and on the other, the investment that the company has made to achieve these earnings.

The first number – the operating profit – can be found in the company's accounts; the second – the capital that is needed to invest to obtain this result – is based on more elaborate information, which can be obtained from the balance sheet.

And how do we get to this invested capital number (assets related to operations)? I will summarise with another question: what money would you put down to generate this return? Well, broadly speaking, you'd be dealing with the following investments: fixed assets (machinery, property, computer equipment, etc.), intangible fixed assets (patents, trademarks, administrative franchises, computer applications and so forth), warehouse stock (inventory), the amount of goods that has been delivered to the customer but still hasn't been charged (commercial debt) and the cash amount in the bank account needed for day-to-day expenditures. All these line items are on the asset side of the balance sheet. Add them up and you will have the amount of operating assets.

However, you will not have to pay this entire amount. Take a look at the liabilities side of the balance sheet and you will see that you have an ally: commercial creditors, creditors that provide you with supplies and services and whose payment is deferred.

Now we have the ingredients. Let's go to the formula:

$$\text{Operating profitability} = \frac{\text{Operating profit}}{\text{Assets related to operations} - \text{Commercial creditors}}$$

Qualitative factors

Not everything is numbers. There are certain aspects of the company that imply greater value beyond ratios. Think of Procter & Gamble, Danone, Nike or Apple, for example. You are willing to pay more to have these brands. Whether it's for their close shave, active yoghurt culture, the comfort and design of their trainers or just the temptation to have a bite of the fruit, you want some of their products.

The objective of these brands is to increase what Warren Buffett calls "moat" day after day. Behind every "moat", there is always a good company.

The degree of the company's diversification and internationalisation corresponds to life insurance. If a company can break out of its local confines and launch itself globally, there is no doubt that its balance sheet will reward it when the domestic market shows signs of fatigue.

Take an interest in the company management, too. Follow their professional careers and analyse the current executive management's previous work, wherever they've been. Let me recommend an indispensable book for a good investor's library: *Common Stocks and Uncommon Profits*, by Philip A. Fisher.

Looking for good entry points

This is what we all want (which is why they're so hard to find). But as investors we all know the keyword: inefficiency.

Inefficiency is this little – sometimes big – market failure that opens up an opportunity to buy or sell. Are there failures in the market? Of course there are.

Thoroughly work up the company's fundamentals, sharpen your investor claws and lie in wait for your chance to pounce. There are no secret formulae. And patience, you need a lot of patience. However, if there is one thing I have learnt, it is that you only learn by investing.

If you buy the same thing that others are buying, you will have the same results as the rest. It is impossible to have better profits if you don't do something different from the majority. Buying when others are selling like crazy and selling when everyone else is senselessly buying has been and will be the most difficult strategy to follow, but also the one that offers the best returns. This is no new idea: Sir John Templeton, one of the most recognised contrarian investors in the world, took note of this some years ago when he suggested the best time to buy was when countries and companies hit "the point of maximum pessimism", and even earlier still, in the 18th century Baron Rothschild, averred: "Buy when there's blood in the streets, even if the blood is your own." Nevertheless, in the end, fear of being left out usually ends up prevailing, and makes it very difficult for investors to defy the status quo. And given the risk of certain peripheral Europe assets, for example, it is absolutely understandable that they will not be found in a traditional institutional investor's portfolio. And yet, the fact that these assets are not in most investors' portfolios doesn't make them riskier, but potentially more profitable.

In my experience, I believe that there are two minimum necessary conditions to be successful in this type of strategy: independence and perfect knowledge of the investment thesis that you are following at all times.

Lastly, I'd like to emphasise that to start managing other people's money you need to apologise ahead of time for the opinionated nature that this requires. In my opinion, your only valid defence is the perfect alignment between the interests of the manager and their investors. The best way of achieving this is for all of the manager's financial wealth to be invested in the same vehicle as the investors'. I don't want to say that what I am saying is the absolute final word. Interpret the world around you and make investment decisions. Sometimes, even full of good faith and concentrating all the forces of the soul, you say "Open sesame!" and the door won't open. Then, you put your hands in your pockets and leave, because there is no reason to be ashamed.

CHAPTER THIRTY-ONE

A STRANGE CASE: COMPANIES WITH POLITICIANS

We spend a lot of time reading news story after news story about politicians of all stripes being appointed to the ranks of companies' management boards and operational areas. Without knocking the unquestionable qualities of our dignitaries and their versatility in quickly becoming experts in all kinds of subjects, the only thing that interests me (as an investor) is knowing whether they create value for the shareholder.

I am afraid that, in many cases (there are exceptions), the contributions of politicians to the value of a company are at best irrelevant, if not negative. This is without taking into account the opportunity cost of not hiring other professionals, or even worse the real cost of discouraging "career" managers to the point of reducing them to the path of least resistance because, "After all, what's the point?"

It's not surprising that, just before the crisis, the "political" stocks started to crash compared to the rest of their sectors. Despite the "strategic" buy decisions, this was when excessive debt began, and ruinous business practices that had been previously hidden among the good ones came to light. It happens with relative frequency with French, Italian and Spanish securities, but also includes some American, English and several Brazilian and Russian ones.

It's important to emphasise that most ex-politicians are appointed to big conglomerates with many businesses, where analysis of the divisions is very difficult because some subsidise others and especially because of the high regulatory burden. It is noticeable, on the other hand, that we've never seen these types of appointments in family-owned or independent companies, where the shareholders have their own wealth on the line and where every euro of investment must generate an adequate return on the cost of capital.

I have found that most of the large companies full of politicians or ex-politicians have consistently underperformed their peers in Europe since 2008.

In addition, independence makes for freedom. I always carry Steve Wynn's (Wynn Resorts) speech with me, where he gave the results from the third quarter of 2011 and freely, publically and harshly criticised the Obama administration. And there are cases like Rex Tillerson of Exxon, who refused to make investments recommended by his government. These are examples of freedom and a lack of favours owed. Let's not forget that there are also exceptions in Spain, and very honourable ones.

If adding politicians to the boards of directors of companies is supposed to defend the interests of the shareholders, why don't we see a higher creation of value than in the other comparable companies? One of investors' concerns is that heavily politicised companies (i.e. semi-state-owned companies prepared to employ many former politicians) tend to get little economic benefit from hiring ex-politicians, as these executives tend to ignore the risks of too much debt when recommending acquisitions. Many times, when a politician comes through the door, value goes out the window.

Comments about semi-governmental and government-controlled enterprises could not be more aggressive. The stock market performance of these "political securities" (semi-state-owned stocks) has traditionally been poor because of various factors:

- Low profitability investment decisions, where companies act like "budget busters". In fact, one of the constants of these securities is that they "invest" way beyond their means, with very low profits, because the different operating areas act like little empires. Look closely and you'll see capital spending (mostly useless "investment" expenditures) shooting up every year between the third and fourth quarter. The political securities, on average, generate returns on capital employed of between 3 and 4% less than comparable securities.
- Acquisitions that destroy value. In general, you will probably read in the newspapers about one "small acquisition" after another, at very high prices and in "high growth" markets that then neither grow nor generate value. These semi-state owned stocks have destroyed no less than €58 billion in value between 2007 and 2012 (Eurostoxx), and have had to write down losses for strategic ventures every three fiscal years.
- The same politicians that are supposedly "defending" the company business also try to use the company's cash flow for "special" interests. There are companies on the brink of bankruptcy which paid up unsustainable dividends that their "leading shareholders" needed. There are also companies who bought completely unrelated businesses to their core competence because of "government suggestions". More than €30 billion in "strategic" acquisitions outside of the core business between 2007 and 2013.
- Total break from the meritocratic model of the company, which makes workers and middle management behave like bureaucrats. Most of these companies have at least two business divisions that generate profits below the cost of capital. Often, when the "professional politicians" enter the business

world, they usually act just like they do in government: they turn a competitive and meritocratic world into a "state office".
- "Creative" objectives. A lot of management by objective that is always achieved and variable compensation that is nothing more than extra pay.
- Top management receives very low compensation percentages in shares. They usually also earn enormous salaries and invest meagre amounts in their own business in comparison to their fixed salaries. It is also strange to see that the board members' pay always goes up, even when results decline. I haven't seen a single company that's been penalised for disastrous or value-destroying investments. It's the long term, Lacalle, the long term.

The interesting thing about these political securities is that their trading prices look cheap and are usually highly recommended by analysts. I say that they "look" cheap because when you see their returns on capital employed and the value added from their acquisitions it makes you cry. And many minority investors get carried away by the "cheap" concept of a low P/E, or worse, of a supposedly high dividend return. Until, that is, they cut the dividends.

The first rule of investing is to avoid "value traps", because there are securities that are cheap because they should be… and they stay cheap. The rule here is "Short on strength, never spend on weakness."

The strangest thing about these companies is seeing their voluminous corporate governance reports and the insufferable sustainability reports. Every time I receive a 600-page pile of paper from a company it goes in the rubbish can, and I buy it short.

It is true that the poor performance always reflects poorly on – and it does – the traditional sayings that "the market doesn't understand us", "it's too short-sighted" or my favourite "the bears get fat on our company", which usually hides management teams that, with few exceptions, have a couple of shares in their own company and astronomical salaries. Or board members who don't have a single share (brace yourselves) because of "corporate governance imperative". As the president of a French company once told me a short time ago: "If we owned a lot of shares, our objectives would not be very stable." No comment.

Every day, there are more international investors who refuse to invest or open short positions in companies where these practices are obvious.

If attracting ex-high-powered politicians to companies creates value, which is possible, I propose compensation tied to real returns for these appointees (net profit added adjusted by debt added) and especially a level of equality of interests between the appointees and the investors of at least 100%. In other words, hire them, but through a "detailed and rigorous" process; pay them a fixed salary equal to middle management and 100% of their variable pay in shares, with a penalty of 10% of their fixed salary for each failed investment proposed.

My favourite "shorts"

This is important to summarise. In a market where investment recommendations are predominantly positive, where stock market corrections are considered anomalies and upward moves are deemed "fundamental", where the mantra of "Do not fight the central banks" is almost religion, we forget that this bullish macroenvironment provides fantastic opportunities to generate alpha with shorts.

Regarding short positions there is a not-surprising widespread myth: it is not easy to find long-term shorts because the risk is asymmetric. That is because even when one finds a Lehman it cannot fall by more than 100%, but stocks can rise much higher.

This is true, but we forget that the role of a short position is not exactly "to go down" but to finance a long position and reduce volatility. And once you have found that stock you love, where you see a huge potential but also a high level of volatility and a significant risk, you can fund that position with a good short. Do not surrender to beta and close your eyes.

In Europe it is rare to find minority investors who finance their long-term good ideas with short positions, but here in the UK or the United States it is very common, and learning to mitigate volatility is part of the success of investment, whether as an individual or as an institution, especially in a market where moves are exaggerated, violent and very short term.

That's why the best things are those gems of shorts that tend to behave worse than their peers over the years.

Forget the ECB, the Bank of Japan, the Fed and the Bank of England. There is a very clear reason why certain companies in selected sectors such as semi-state-owned electric utilities, telecommunications, some integrated oil companies, construction and concessionaires tend to underperform their indexes: value destruction through the investment process. Companies spend money to generate lower returns: running to a standstill. These are the jewel shorts, and bullish market environments create "short on strength, never buy on weakness" opportunities.

As I said before, when you read an analyst's report, the three sentences that will alert you to a possible short, a company of value-destroying qualities, are when you read "It's a good company," "Fundamentals have not changed" or "Dividend yield is high."

Use the ratio of EV/IC/ROIC/WACC, which measures how expensive a stock is relative to its investment process. If the company generates an ROIC (return on invested capital) that is lower than its WACC (weighted average cost of capital) and the enterprise value (EV: market cap plus debt and financial commitments) exceeds its invested capital (IC, including provisions and "write-offs"), then the stock is more expensive even if the shares have fallen in the market.

A value trap tends to destroy shareholder value through megalomaniac "diversification" acquisitions, which analysts and management always consider "small", or through large capital expenditure programmes with very poor returns. These are companies that, through the process of making acquisitions and investing, become "fatter" not "stronger".

Similarly, there are stocks that are expensive and deserve to be so. Companies that create true value become more expensive without the need for acquisitions or mergers; they are expensive because they are more profitable, stronger and because they focus on what they actually do well.

These "value traps" usually follow a vicious circle: The companies are "pro-cyclical". They buy high when the market is "hot" and sell low when debt drowns them. Acquisitions are made at steep multiples for alleged "growth" markets or to "diversify" – if they have to diversify, it is because something is wrong with their core business.

They always "invest" late. These are companies with multi-billion capital expenditure plans that are almost always targeted at copying what their leading competitors do, creating a bubble in which everyone participates, until it explodes. And afterwards come the downgrades of the company's own estimates ... the profit warnings, the capital increases and convertible bonds ... without costing anyone their job.

This cycle always leads to excessive debt, because the "growth" always disappoints and because margins deteriorate. It starts with justifications – "we can afford it" – then continues with shareholder-dilutive actions (convertible bonds, issuance of preferred stock or hybrids) and ends with write-offs, dividend cuts and capital increases at rock-bottom prices.

Back to acquisitions "to grow" and press "reset". There will always be some CEO who will say to you that the "shares do not reflect the real value of the company", that the "new plan is different and very realistic" and that "the fundamentals have not changed".

CHAPTER THIRTY-TWO

COMMUNICATION WITH THE MARKET AND ATTRACTIVENESS TO INVESTORS

"This company has a communication problem," said a high-level executive upon seeing shares slide another 2% after already sinking 21%. "What it has, is a profits and credibility problem," I dared to say. You could have cut the air with a knife. A company can have the best channels of communication, the most modern webpage and the most luxurious strategic presentations in the most exotic places, but if there is no sustainable income or adequate profitability, it won't work.

The job of a financial communication professional is not easy. If the share is doing well, the management team gives themselves a pat on the back. If not, there's a "communication problem". In this chapter I'd like to pay tribute to my former co-workers in the area of investor and media relations, those heroes and heroines who work so hard to inform the world about the company. I had the privilege and luck to work with high-level executives who valued and supported such an essential function in publicly traded companies. Nevertheless, we've all heard anecdotes of nights waiting for the new strategic presentation or the latest updates from the president or chief executive, of races to the work centre to change a slide that the financial director finally decided to include, of the hundreds of comments relayed back over each event or results publication in these companies where there are so many cooks for so little broth. And my favourite: "Why did the share fall today after all the good work we did?" I salute you all.

Spanish companies, for example, went through an admirable process of adaptation at the end of the nineties, and it has been no easy feat that today they are much better regarded by investors than they were 10 years ago. Year after year, various presidents and investor relationship teams receive some of the highest votes in the prestigious awards from Institutional Investor, *IR Magazine* and Thomson Extel. In addition, they have achieved this through a process of internationalisation and expansion that was implemented during the middle of three huge crises: the Latin American crisis between 1999 and 2001, the 2008 financial crisis and the European crisis. Reaching this point in such a complex environment deserves recognition. But they cannot become self-satisfied. I would like to highlight some of the elements needing improvement.

The financial world has changed radically since I started. On one hand, information is now controlled by hundreds of alternative channels rather than companies. Shareholder activism and social media are adding a new level. Companies are more active... and so are shareholders.

On the other, investors no longer focus on 10 or 12 securities. We are almost all global investors, and the ability to synthesise and use time has become an essential element in the management of portfolios.

The world of investment has also changed. Today, active management predominates over passive, the indexed funds are no longer as important as before and the maturation period for a variable income investment has been significantly reduced. Even "long only" are invested for a shorter time than previously. In addition, more attention is being paid to fixed income, changes in credit variables and macroeconomic indicators.

In this environment, hedge funds form a very relevant part of the whole institutional investor world and the one that is most combative, critical and active. As a result, they have an important influence on the orientation of corporate communication.

From my point of view, the big mistakes that companies make in their approach to communication are centred on four big areas:

- Thinking that "less is better". Concealing information, not breaking down the accounts, hiding divisions and changing reporting methods does not help: it weakens perceptions of worth and increases distrust.
- Obsessing over buy recommendations. Amassing a large amount of buy recommendations doesn't mean anything. As I will come on to later, it can even be negative, since it often denotes an excessive influence from the company on recommendations.
- Focusing communication efforts on the long-term and passive funds and ignoring those that have a more relevant influence on value, which are active funds and marginal investments. But above all, they should take care of short investors in the security. Convincing the bears is much more efficient, and the company will learn more about its strengths and weaknesses.

Another essential element when communicating strategy to hedge funds and active investors is to pay attention to the balance sheet. While companies are focused on debt over operating results, the key resides in also giving information about something that few companies analyse: the deterioration of working capital, in other words the amount of capital debt that the company has to put out in order to stay afloat in a period of recession.

The reason why hedge funds increase bearish positions in some companies, including when shares are going up, is because the companies' costs of "surviving" are shooting up and they are not doing anything to keep them in check. With an annual necessity ratio of working capital that in various cases means 20% of sales (working capital/sales), these securities are given the name of "the living dead" in the market as it costs more to maintain the activity than to stop it.

The investor relations team has the duty of informing its management which ratios the investors really care about, and making them see that investors are increasingly less tolerant of messages that "mislead and conceal". I remember a conversation with a big institutional investor who told me that "wasting time also makes me decide to sell". Investors are demanding better quality and more detail in the information that they receive. If we add to this the enormous complexity that the companies introduce in their accounts for corporate operations, it is important that communication focus on avoiding the "conglomerate discount". Investors are not mind readers, so if a company makes their analysis complicated or difficult, makes purchases without providing pro forma data sheets, changes divisions or reorganises its way of reporting, the market immediately applies a discount. This discount has done nothing but increase over the last few years (in some cases up to 35% on the sum of the parts), as investors have started seeing the strategic "promises" vanish. Chief executives and financial officers don't like it and don't accept it, but that is how it is and how it will continue to be. The excuse that the "market is not informed" indicates paternalism and arrogance. It is the company that has to make an effort at communication since it is competing for the investors' capital, not the other way around.

I referred before to the valuation of the sum of the parts that many companies use to suggest that their shares are cheap when they see their multiples are being squeezed. This is a strategy that doesn't work, because this sum of the parts includes purchased assets and is also usually irrelevant in companies that are not for sale or that, precisely through the diversification purchases, have filled the security with "poison pills". "Poison pills" are all those things that artificially shield a company from possible purchase by making it complicated or unattractive to the buyer.

In order for a corporate strategy to work and the security to be seen as a good medium- to long-term investment, and not a short position, we need to consider a few factors, some which are in the hands of the companies and others which are not. These factors are the macroeconomic environment, benign investment and a strategy that is genuinely oriented towards total profitability for the shareholder, which doesn't depend mainly on the economic cycle but on the company's own management capability and expenditure control.

Nevertheless, when communicating, it's worth focusing on three points:

• What is the company acting on today? Despite strategic mistakes, particularly value-destroying ones like "acquisitions in order to diversify", many companies are showing that they manage their main business incredibly well. If they contain their working capital and focus on the area where they have true ability to act, the market will reward them.

- A commitment not to go back to the mistake of "diversifying", or growing for the sake of growing. The market rewards those who learn from their mistakes. Reducing size and becoming a cash-making machine by letting the balance sheet breathe is more attractive in the medium term. Focused and efficient companies are worth a lot more than dysfunctional conglomerates.
- Commitment to transparency. Nobody will appreciate debt reduction if it is the product of financial engineering. So don't even try it. Investors will buy when the margins, cash flow and balance sheets recover, not from changes in accounting criteria.

There's nothing I like more as an investor than a security where there are a lot of short positions, analysts' recommendations are neutral or negative and it's in the process of rapidly and efficiently recovering. These are stock market treasures. And there is nothing I like more to buy short than a security that tries to disguise its balance sheets and cash flow while its working capital shoots up, its returns plummet and there are a lot of buy recommendations piling up. These are the "short on strength" diamonds that gave us so much joy in 2008 and 2011.

While many executives and directors are obsessed with getting a lot of buy recommendations and congratulating themselves for adding income through purchases, the market appreciates reality: cash flow, margins and balance sheets, not imperialist ventures. In my time in the area of investor relations, it was clear to me that there was nothing better than putting a company in the black where it mattered, in other words in terms of its ROCE and its balance sheet. Focus your communication efforts on those who, for now, don't want to buy or are buying short, not on those you already have, who are the first to sell in this market. You will learn a lot.

CHAPTER THIRTY-THREE

WHY INVEST IN A HEDGE FUND?

With hedge funds, like any other investment product, you have to look around and compare. For example, profits in small funds are usually higher than the big ones, and there is more frequent contact between investors and managers and the relationship is more open. The three big requirements for investing in a hedge fund must be: low volatility, low correlation and liquidity. I would add an intangible but extremely important objective to this: constant dialogue with the managers.

When we talk about alternative management, I like to focus on neutral investment in the market. I'm not interested in directional strategies. I don't need a manager to play at "everything is going up" and "the fundamentals haven't changed" or "everything is down because it's going bad". It doesn't make sense to give money to managers who justify bad investments when their strategy is supposed to be well covered.

In 2011, the hedge fund industry attracted $51 billion in capital at a global level. In 2011 alone, 1,100 new hedge funds were launched into the world. In 2012, the industry brought in $80 billion and launched another 1,000 funds. In 2013, the industry broke the $2 trillion barrier and added 1,500 new firms. Eighty-one per cent applied neutral strategies in shares and credit, according to HSBC. I will focus my comments on this segment, which is the one I move in and where I see the greatest potential.

A common mistake is thinking that alternative management funds charge excessive commissions. Averages are misleading for analysing hedge funds' commissions. If you take enormous funds or any of the high-commission funds (which charge between 3 and 10% management commission) and add in those which charge only 1.5%, the average gets skewed. Actually, non-directional management funds are a bargain compared to those charged by traditional investment managers. The reason is very simple. As an investor, if I am going to absorb volatility of 25 to 30%, paying 1% commission could be too high. That is when paying a 1.5% management fee is worth it for getting volatility of less than 15% and double-digit annual returns in serious non-directional funds. The most important thing is managing at low volatility and low market correlation.

Averages are misleading when it comes to talking about heterogeneous companies. And to talk about hedge funds in general is like talking about pension funds in general. This is simply a group based on a very limited common element, the use of leveraged positions. However, strategies vary widely and the results are obviously disparate depending on how much risk, directionality and volatility the client accepts for each fund. This last point is very important. Every fund has a very different volatility rate, net market exposure and liquidity objectives.

This is where the most positive aspect of the alternative investment industry is seen: it is totally aggressive. Only the best survive, which is the opposite of what happens with passive or index-based management. The manager shares the risk with the investor, because the manager usually has all their money invested in their own fund.

In my view, the reasons for investing in a hedge fund are:

- Much higher returns than "conservative" products in the medium term, and good returns in the short. As much as risk is criticised, the most neutral strategies have generated returns of between 15 and 20% annually, including the two worst years of 2008 and 2011.
- Take advantage of periods of high-capital attraction to invest in very favourable commission terms relative to the volatility involved. Most neutral funds charge a 1.5% management commission and a 20% commission only if an agreed minimum profit (high watermark) is achieved.
- Greater alignment of interests between managers and investors. Would you prefer your money to be managed by some guy with a fixed salary or someone who is putting all their capital on the line with you?
- Liquidity and transparency tied to short-term results. This is very important, because access to your money as an investor must be guaranteed, and strategies that invest in non-liquid assets like micro-businesses or assets not traded on exchanges usually carry more short-term risk.
- The ability to create a portfolio with less risk and volatility by investing in various alternative sectorial funds depending on the investor's interests, as opposed to the basket offered by some passive managers.
- The use of technology to establish an open dialogue with the manager, not only through their monthly reports.
- A market with interest rates that will continue being low (and where governments are destroying their currencies by printing money) makes leveraged and active strategies more attractive.
- A break with the passive management model. In an economy that is moving between mini-crisis and short periods of expansion and contraction, active management is more relevant than ever.

- Ability to move assets at a global level. To be able to invest in any part of the world reduces exposure to macroeconomic risks without requiring the manager to step aside because their mandate is to invest in specific assets.

It's no surprise that, in the face of an economy where governments destroy currencies, create lower interest rates and burden the system with debt, many investors use these disadvantageous policies to increase their exposure to hedge funds.

This is a good time to take advantage of this increase in assets under management, to start to diversify with more complex and attractive products and to provide access to an industry where the investor can find transparency, open dialogue and liquidity, and demand the utmost from their manager.

CHAPTER THIRTY-FOUR

TEN GOLDEN RULES FOR INVESTING

The best ideas I have always come from not listening to everybody else.

Trader's comment

Not long ago, I saw an episode of *Bonanza* (1960) on economic bubbles. At one point in the episode, Lorne Green, the father of the Cartwrights, mentions to one of his sons: "Stay out of the market unless you want to see yourself buried in worthless paper." Nothing has changed since then. Nevertheless, we keep creating economic and stock-market bubbles. It is essential not to fall into them, or at least not to stay within them when they crash.

I think that it's important to distil what I have mentioned in these chapters into 10 golden rules for investing, while knowing that there are always times when we make mistakes, but that these mistakes are the most important things to learn from. Learn from your mistakes; don't brag about your successes.

1. **Buy what you know.** There isn't a security that can't be summarised in three sentences. Note their main characteristics in terms of profit generation, what the consensus expects from the security and what you suspect others don't know. And follow this to the letter. If you don't understand the balance sheets, where supplies come from, what the real risk exposure is, what the sustainable margins are or why the companies are not making more money when the economy is growing, don't invest.

2. **If you're buying growth, don't keep a share in your portfolio for value and then hold on to it for dividends.** Self-deception is the worst thing possible. If a security looks like a good opportunity for growth and then it turns out that it isn't, don't hold on to it because it's "cheap", or later, when it falls even more, because of its dividends. Recognising mistakes is crucial. This is especially true, because this type of spectacular growth can be an indicator of a bubble. When it bursts, the share's bottom can be a lot lower than you think.

3. **Look closely at numbers, not commentaries.** General and vague comments like "It's a very diversified company with a lot of overseas assets" are obvious and already known and taken into account as part of the forecasts of the financial world; on the other hand, comments like "The traditional valuation ratios don't work for this type of security" indicate that it's very likely that you are looking at a bubble that is about to burst. Pay close attention to the numbers, the profits and the balance sheet and analyse whether they correspond to your risk profile.

4. **Recommendations are free; the losses are yours.** Analyse securities and investments from your own information and perspective. Listen to the opinions of others, if you want, but always take them for what they are: opinions. If everything goes badly, the one with the recommendations will tell you "the fundamentals haven't changed", and you will still be losing money.

5. **Think about how much you stand to lose before you think about how much you could gain.** It's not easy, but do a risk–benefit analysis. It's not a bad idea to start on the basis that consensus analysts tend to overestimate companies' future profits by 10 to 12% on average. If we assume a potential loss of 20% in a year, for example, the potential gain should be at least 40% to make the risk–benefit ratio attractive. Always invest your extra money. Emergencies and liquidity are not good options when it comes to investing. When you invest, even if it's in fixed income or something that you consider very safe, be clear that you stand to lose a lot of money.

6. **If you are thinking long term, scale your positions.** If you invest with the perspective of various years, have some back-up to be able to increase positions in case of bad times. If not, you won't get anything from the "rebounds"; you'll just mitigate your losses.

7. **Watch out for the "bigger fool theory"** that "the Chinese, the Russians, the Germans are going to come and buy this or that", or worse, "this is so cheap that it's going to be bought by a predator any minute". Be careful about thinking that a corporate rumour is true, because most of the time it isn't and it contains more risks than potential benefits. Buy something that is worth more for you as an independent company according to your own estimates. If it is acquired afterwards, all the better, but don't let it be your central thesis. The predators (acquirers) are rarely fools.

8. **There are securities that are cheap because they should be.** Be careful with "value traps". A security that was trading at P/E 12 and now trades at 8 doing the same business, having the same results and the same management team can contain a value trap that is going to lose money for you because the company is destroying value

for the shareholder through self-indulgent purchases (they'll always tell you that these are "small") or through unnecessary investments with very poor returns. There are also expensive securities that become more expensive. Companies that create real value become more expensive without acquisitions or mergers; they become more expensive because they are more profitable, stronger and because they focus on what they do really well.

9. **Buy a security for what it is, not for what the management team or the banks would like it to be.** We tend to highlight areas or divisions that in many cases are irrelevant because they are not the ones that generate most of the company's profits. This is logical for sellers, but the buyer should know, just like when you buy a moisturising cream that you know is 80% water, that in many companies 80% of the impact in the security can be due to what people don't like to talk about because it's not "sexy".

10. **Alignment of corporate and shareholder interests.** Why is it that the companies which do best in the stock market are often the ones where the managers receive a very high percentage of their compensation in company securities or are the owners of the majority stakes? Because they take care of the money that they are spending. Try to distinguish between manager-entrepreneurs who are majority owners in their business and manager-VIP employees who may create a lot of value in some cases but may also just be fuelling their ego with the shareholders' money.

CHAPTER THIRTY-FIVE

"WARNING" PHRASES AND COMMENTS

One of the most important and useful courses I've ever taken in my life was given by Business Intelligence Advisors, a consulting firm founded by ex-CIA and United States government agents that teaches you how to recognise and understand when someone is lying or being deceptive. We were taught to read behaviour and changes in attitude models and to analyse those phrases, verbal or written that could be a warning that something was not right. Along with the Master's degree from IESE, this was the most valuable training I've received since I started working.

When you visit hundreds of companies, receive thousands of calls from analysts and banks and a ton of recommendation emails, the information overload can be unbearable. It is extremely useful to have tools available to try to recognise where there may be mistakes or questions. My son Pablo, who is an avid reader and film fan, always says that "the book explains it better", and when he goes to the cinema in Spain to see a film in its original language he says that "what they are saying is not what they put in the subtitles". The financial market is not much different. You need to try to be properly informed, so as not to be persuaded by others whose opinions may not necessarily be rooted in fact. You need to try to read between the lines and not be misled by the scripted summary and "subtitles".

We've already talked about the three phrases of determining whether a security can be a good short position: "The fundamentals haven't changed", "It's a good company" and "It offers good dividends." Then there are classics like: "It's all already been taken into account", when the market has shown us that an event is rarely totally taken into account or "My forecasts are very conservative", when we've been revising forecasts downwards for each of the last five years by 10–12%.

After almost 10 years in the financial world, I've written down some of the strangest, most shocking phrases and comments that I've heard from analysts as well as companies and managers:

- "No one owns this stock" (Me: "It is 100% owned every day") "You know what I mean" (Me: "No, I don't"). It is a very typical trick to try to sell a security by saying, "Nobody owns it." First of all, this is not true and, second, it assumes that the fact that there are few buyers is an unjustified anomaly that will be corrected in the medium term.
- "The company has to take a $4bn write-off, which would be very positive for returns." This is an attempt to sell negative news (acknowledging losses) as something positive. Of course, if the company can provide for 100% of its shares, it will have infinite profitability.
- "Why would you think that a state-owned company would not increase tariffs by 20%?" Sometimes we think that semi-government companies or those which are subject to interventions are going to operate according to market criteria. This is a mistake.

- "If you forget the sovereign and macro concerns, it is very cheap" (tied with "We leave that to the strategists" and "On an absolute basis, the stock is cheap"). As if the macroeconomic factors like growth possibility and regulatory and tax risks were something like bad weather that doesn't have an impact on the company's cost of capital.
- "I'm only concerned about the fundamentals, not sovereign risk" – another great phrase.
- "The 'overhang' doesn't matter because it provides a chance to buy cheaper." This is another way of putting an optimistic halo on a problem. An "overhang" occurs when there is a significant percentage of majority investors who must sell.
- "It has a very high dividend yield" (Me: "The 10-year sovereign bond gives a higher yield.") "Why is that significant?" When a sovereign bond goes up exponentially, the country risk and dividend yield increase, meaning the security isn't well supported even if the company has a good dividend. This would mean assuming that there is no risk differential between variable and fixed income.
- "We recommend buying this security even though we've lowered our forecasts by 20%." No comment.
- "Semi-government companies have less risk because the governments will never let them fail"… or let them create value for the shareholders.
- "We recommend buying. The valuation of the multiples look expensive at first, but we don't think it really is because the company's accounting methods are not reliable." Really? Recommending buying a company whose accounting methods are questionable?
- "We recommend buying. The excessive debt of the group doesn't concern us because we are interested in the equity, not its bonds." Great, call me the day it goes bankrupt to see how the shares respond.

Some of my favourite phrases from meeting with companies are:

- "We didn't do a 'profit warning': it's a prudent revision of forecasts" (a profit warning is when the company revises its earnings and objectives forecasts downwards in the short or medium term) or, "The company today is an opportunity to buy for the very long-term investor." Sometimes very, very long-term.
- "The management team owns few shares in the company, because if they buy a lot it could be seen as affecting their long-term view", which can be easily translated to "We're making a killing on our fixed salary and bonuses, we're destroying value and we'd like you to pay for the fall we're taking in the market."
- "This acquisition has not destroyed value. That depends on your definition of value." I was told this by a company that, after spending $40 billion in acquisitions, reduced its earnings by 34%. Their managers created a lot of value… in their own pockets. Their salaries increased by 12%.
- "This company has never reduced its dividends. Paying the dividend in shares is proof of our commitment." This was uttered to me by a company that spent four years paying dividends in shares hence diluting its own shareholders.
- "A convertible bond is not dilutive, because the shares will go up a lot in the long term." The clairvoyance of managers about the value of their shares in the long term is only comparable to their lack of commitment to the security in the short term.
- "Of course, we are staying with our targets, we've only revaluated them." Meaning, they've been revised downwards.
- "Our plan hasn't changed; it has only been postponed by the crisis." Another big phrase where "the crisis" is a kind of UFO

that came out of nowhere and wasn't taken into account in the "very conservative" forecasts.

- "Debt doesn't affect the fundamentals." No, it only sinks them. Or another favourite saying: "The write-downs don't affect the company's earnings." Yes, right. The write-downs represent acknowledgement of losses precisely because of the company's lack of profitability.
- "The long-term will show we are right," said a company whose value fell from €70 per share to €12 per share in three years. The long-term is getting longer. No manager was fired.
- "You can't judge the value of a company just from its earnings and balance sheet." No, sure: the valuation is judged by how pretty its office buildings are.
- But my favourite all-time saying, the crown jewel, was from an Italian company: "We are committed to the objective of having the highest dividend yields in the sector." The dividend yield is the dividend per share divided by the share price. Among other things, the dividend yield can go up... if the price of the share falls. The company achieved its objective and reached a dividend yield of 12%, because the share fell by 45%. Congratulations, an unforgettable sentence.

Everyone makes mistakes in this world. We shouldn't forget to mention the most shocking sayings of friends and competitors in fund management and what, in my opinion, they really mean:

- "The market is wrong": I'm wrong.
- "At these levels, I am keeping the position due to valuation": I made a mistake and this disaster that I bought with inflated growth forecasts now has fallen too much for me to admit my mistake.
- "It's only a correction": I'm losing money and have to convince the others not to sell.

- "It has a lot of catalysts": There's no point looking at it on multiples, because it's way too expensive.
- "The feeling of the market is clearly bullish, but nervous": I have no idea what people are thinking.
- "The security is at historic support levels": I'm up to my neck in losses in this share, please buy some.
- "If I were you, I would buy this share": If I were me, I'd sell them to you.
- "The management team is doing what it can": The results are going to be pitiful.
- "It has all been discounted": I'm swimming in loss-making shares and here comes one more piece of bad news.
- "I'm having a good year if you compare it to the indices": I'm losing… but others are doing worse.

CHAPTER THIRTY-SIX

BOOKS AND FILMS ABOUT THE MARKET

I love film and books, and more than anything I am a big music fan. Over the years I've been making personal lists of books, films and songs that I've mentioned in *El Confidencial* and that have helped me better understand this world I work in. The book that has most affected me on the world of hedge funds is *More Money than God: Hedge Funds and the Making of a New Elite*, by Sebastian Mallaby, a book that talks about the great managers and their importance in the financial sphere while providing a critical and original analysis. I consider it absolutely essential for anyone who wants to enter this world. Another essential book for understanding hedge funds, which analyses (and actually predicted) the mortgage crisis and the excesses of the banks, is *The Big Short* by Michael Lewis.

The book that most showed me how to understand the global economy and put the current crisis into context is *This Time is Different: Eight Centuries of Financial Folly* by Carmen Reinhart and Ken Rogoff, an indispensable guide for everyone who says that the current crisis is without comparison and that the previous system was better and more controlled. It shows that for seven hundred years the world has had economic cycles of expansion and recession, in many cases more severe than this one. To understand the history of the 1929 crisis and the mistakes that were made, the best book is *The Lords of Finance: The Bankers Who Broke the World*, by Liaquat Ahamed. To understand the mistakes and consequences of the suicidal expansionist policy of the central banks and their effects, especially the creation of artificial bubbles, *The Origin of Financial Crises: Central Banks, Credit Bubbles and the Efficient Market Fallacy* by George Cooper is worth a read.

When small investors and readers ask me about possible guides for good investing practices, I think that by far the best book is one that debunks the myths we've been used to hearing for decades and still hear on the radio and television. This book is called *The 12 Investment Myths: Why Individual Investors are Failing Miserably and How You Can Avoid Being One of Them* by Jack Calhoun. And we mustn't forget the Bible on bonds: *Bond Markets, Analysis and Strategies* by Frank J. Fabozzi, and two essential books for understanding the energy market: *The Prize: The Epic Quest for Oil, Money, and Power* and *The Quest: Energy, Security, and the Remaking of the Modern World* by Daniel Yergin.

I will now follow with my favourite films for understanding the economy. There are many movies on the financial world, from *Wall Street* to *Inside Job* and *Margin Call*, but my favourites are basically the following.

At a time when social rights, emigration, evictions and the role of banks are almost daily headlines, *The Grapes of Wrath* (1940, John Ford) and *It's A Wonderful Life* (1946, Frank Capra) are two masterpieces that show us how things have changed very little. Their subjects and messages are more relevant today than ever.

In my opinion, among the better movies on the world of the stock market is *The Boiler Room* (2000, Ben Younger), which perfectly illustrates the culture of the more aggressive brokers and sellers from the perspective of a shady company.

Wall Street (1987, Oliver Stone) will be remembered for all time for its character Gordon Gekko and his speech "Greed is good", but from my point of view the film that best reflects the environment of greed and excess of the eighties is *American Psycho* (2000, Mary Harron). Based on Bret Easton Ellis' excellent novel, this uses the absolutely brilliant metaphor of an investment banker who is also at the same time a serial killer. It likens the egoism of that period and culture with a psychopath's disdain for people. If you also read the book, it's worth noting the chapters where the protagonist talks about music and where his schizophrenic personality comes through in something as innocent as his analysis of the recordings of Whitney Houston or Genesis.

Moving on to the corporate world, one of my favourite films on the subject is *Glengarry Glen Ross* (1992, David Mamet). This is an adaptation of a great play by the same director, which was made into a beautiful and tough film about the corporate world and competition inside a real estate firm. Alec Baldwin, who plays the unscrupulous despotic boss, Blake, and Jack Lemmon, the salesman looking for his last chance to show that he still has it, are exceptional. They have feigned conversations with supposedly interested buyers who really just want some company and conversation. As examples of salesmen telling their war stories, these are just as important as any examples of gripes from the corporate world.

Blake: "As you all know, first prize is a Cadillac Eldorado. Anybody want to see second prize? Second prize is a set of steak knives. Third prize is you're fired."

Another is *Office Space* (1999, Mike Judge). It's without a doubt the best critique I've seen of the day-to-day workings of an office and its typical characters (the useless boss, Gary Cole, exceptional) and the contrived relationship between workers in a disheartening environment.

In the IESE Master's programme, Professor Santiago Álvarez de Mon did a fantastic class on management, leadership and labour relations by using the movie *Crimson Tide* (1995, Tony

Scott) as an example. To this day, I still consider it a manual for management and negotiation that everybody should analyse. It includes an entire economic and strategic organisation, right and wrong choices and decision-making under pressure. Gene Hackman is as excellent as ever.

I am dedicating the last big group of films on the economy to those which, in my opinion, illustrate essential aspects of the United States and the capitalist system. *Trading Places* (1983, John Landis) is a little gem and a great metaphor for America, the economic culture of success, social prejudices and the myths and contradictions of an entire system. It is masterfully done by Landis through not only the two leading characters (Eddie Murphy and Dan Aykroyd) but also through secondary ones, who explain capitalism better than many books. Denholm Elliott, the efficient and obedient butler, Jamie Lee Curtis, the prostitute who invests her earnings in bonds and Ralph Bellamy and Don Ameche, the brilliant multi-millionaire brothers and founders of Duke & Duke, who make sociological wagers without worrying about the harm they cause to people. The scene where the Duke brothers explain to newcomer Eddie Murphy how the commodities market works is fantastic:

"Tell him the good part."

"The good part, William, is that no matter whether our clients make money or lose money, Duke & Duke get their commissions."

I will close this section with one of my all-time favourites. *There Will Be Blood* (2007, Paul Thomas Anderson) is an absolute masterpiece on the creation and development of one of the most important industries in the world: the oil industry. It includes a very critical and detailed analysis of all the segments involved: industry, land and even religion.

The line: "My straw reaches across the room and starts to drink your milkshake... I drink your milkshake! I drink it up!" marvellously sums up the oil industry's policy of expansion and the rise of the big multinationals in the industry.

CHAPTER THIRTY-SEVEN

A DAY IN THE LIFE OF AN INVESTMENT FUND

I've received hundreds of questions about the financial industry over the years. I know that there are a great many myths about the hedge fund sector and hope that the following will clear up some misconceptions about it.

One of the most common questions is what type of investors the sector has. Basically, high-net-worth individuals, pension funds and sovereign funds invest in hedge funds. To receive information about a fund or to be able to invest in one, the investor must be considered a "qualified investor", meaning they have a sophisticated and detailed level of financial knowledge. An investor is considered qualified by legal consultants of the fund on the basis of requirements established by regulatory agencies like the FCA or the SEC. Each fund is explained in detail in its brochure.

A client's relationship with the fund managers depends on what they ask for. All funds publish an informational bulletin with a weekly or monthly analysis of the portfolio. They have investor relations departments that answer questions, and in some cases have periodic conference calls with the fund managers (who are usually open to any enquiry).

The minimum amount for investing in a hedge fund is about $500,000, which can also provide a "filter" for the type of investor who can access these products. They're not for just anybody.

It should be emphasised that the regulatory bodies are extremely strict, which contrasts with the false image of alternative funds operating without regulation. The perception that this is a non-regulated market of cowboys is incorrect. The FCA, the SEC, internal compliance controls and the investors themselves perform detailed analysis of everything that is done.

For example, managers can't make personal investments on a whim. Every time one wants to make a private investment, we have to ask for permission from compliance. This authorisation must be in writing and given prior to carrying out the investment.

For the services they render, funds charge a management fee of between 1.5 and 3.0%, and a performance fee of between 15 and 20%. The crisis has not changed these commissions much, or the minimum investment amounts. Some funds have lowered their commissions, to make them more competitive or to keep in line with new products, but the minimum amounts will still be approximately the same.

There are a lot of fund categories, but it's common to differentiate them by size. A middle-sized fund handles about $500 million to $2 billion. The small ones go from $100 million to $500 million. Normally, the level of independence and freedom for the manager to invest in different sectors and types of products is greater in the medium and small funds, since (unlike the large funds) there are no sector specialists. Investors have less contact with managers in big firms.

The figures for assets under management often mislead large portions of the public, who sometimes think that all this money is being moved around every day. Nevertheless, in a normal day, it is reasonable to expect that funds operate by buying and selling 1% of their total (3% maximum). Very few funds move more than 5% of their assets daily.

Returns vary. People often ask if profitability changes drastically depending on the assets under management. Historically, medium-sized funds are the most profitable, because the managers have more ability to manoeuvre: managing a multi-billion-dollar fund is like moving a cargo tanker, and the most successful large ones diversify by having many managers. As to the number of employees in a fund, this depends on the strategy and level of specialisation. There is no magic number of employees. A medium-sized fund of $1 billion may hire three or four managers and 25–30 professional analysts.

The managers of the hedge funds have a large percentage of their personal money invested in their own fund. This also occurs in traditional funds. Most investments are done using proprietary analysis, although managers also use reports from banks and consultants. Trading is done using different brokers, who charge a commission. This is how bank services are paid.

The analysis and decision-making as to which securities go into a portfolio are both a process of elimination. Some funds analyse an average of six new companies monthly. If they don't like them, they don't invest, but this doesn't mean that they don't follow their returns or that the companies won't later make the list of likely investments. Normally, the complete process of analysing a new security lasts a month from the time of creating a valuation model to the decision as to whether to buy or sell. Each analyst monitors about 250 to 300 companies, of which no more than 20 to 30 end up in the portfolio.

I think it is important to emphasise that the managers are not the only ones responsible for what goes into or comes out of the portfolio. The analysts work at analysing and taking down information.

Managers normally analyse a macroeconomic environment or sector where they see potential. Once decided to invest in something, they look for companies that are well positioned to either benefit from or be disadvantaged by the macroenvironment.

Meeting the executives of the companies is important, not just for the information they provide, which is always publicly available, but also to get an idea of their personality, of how they see the world, to analyse their reactions to certain kinds of questions, to know their opinions on general subjects, etc.

Once managers have analysed a company at a basic level, they also use technical analysis as an additional tool. For example, indicators showing if a stock is oversold or over-bought, its relative strength and DeMark. For me, technical analysis is very useful as a secondary tool, but I am as much against using it as the only tool as I am against ignoring it altogether.

The objectives of a good portfolio are maintaining control and monitoring good ideas, learning to cut losses, accepting that there will be investments that don't work and creating a portfolio that can increase in size. To do this, it is best to avoid aggressive directional positions as much as possible.

Traders can be managers or simply executors. That is when they don't take positions or decide when to get in or get out. These traders only give their opinion on what they think in terms of direction and volatility. They buy and sell what managers choose and indicate to them. But this changes depending on different styles, and there are some hedge funds where the traders have a very specific role in generating profits with market flows.

The trading platforms, in any case, are the same for all the funds: brokers, direct market access … there are no privileges or advantages for one fund or another for accessing liquidity.

In a normal day, a manager works from (for example) about seven in the morning until the United States' markets close, at half nine UK time. This doesn't mean being shut in the office for all this time. BlackBerrys and iPads allow one to work in any place at any time. Work is being done as long as the market is open. Even when managers are on holiday or travelling, they're always checking their email.

Internal meetings are essential for discussing ideas, but managers tend to be in direct contact all the time and make decisions on the hoof. They don't need to sit down for a discussion to make decisions about a security. They are instantaneous. Travel depends on whether it is deemed necessary.

Managers spend about 35% of their time in a typical week seeing or visiting companies and analysts. They typically see about six or seven companies every five days. Approximately 50% of the time is spent reviewing portfolios and buying and selling, and the remaining 15% writing down ideas and strategies for discussion and debate with other managers.

In the first fund I worked in, I quickly learnt to manage my time as efficiently as possible, since I went from covering six companies to 150.

To me, the single key to success in work is doing what you enjoy. And I love this job. Indeed, in the 10 years that I've spent in the hedge fund industry, I have only found great friends and competitors, companionship, understanding and collaboration.

Another myth about alternative management is that it's a "man's world". There are great female managers and analysts. There is a list of the fifty most powerful women in the hedge fund world in the *Hedge Fund Journal* and some of them have, with great consistency, achieved some of the best returns in the market.

The main advantage of dealing with these types of professionals every day is that you get to learn from people who are always saying or analysing something interesting, and this helps you to question your views and to try to improve.

You learn something every day from others, from what concerns them and how they see the economic reality. We all talk about our successes and failures. It's a relaxed and some-times fun atmosphere. I've never seen unfair competition among managers. The only competition I've seen is trying to generate higher returns.

While it may seem like an aggressive world (and it certainly is in part), it doesn't create elite groups. There are better and worse managers and, in general, everybody collaborates and competes against themselves and others. But there are no advantages to backstabbing, because even the best managers in the world have bad days and bad streaks.

Economic compensation is basically focused on the variable part, the productivity bonus and returns. Fixed salaries are higher in investment banks. They are usually very low in hedge funds, and most of the wage is linked to returns. When I read criticisms of the "bonus culture" and the way the investment funds pay workers, I always say that it's a very specific form of compensation for an industry where the client requires results and profits.

When you invest in a fund, you want the managers to work for their money with the utmost responsibility, diligence and risk control. There is no better way of paying them than with a salary tied to their results. This guarantees that managers work hard for their money.

The vast majority of hedge funds are based in the United States and the United Kingdom, followed by Geneva and Sin-gapore, but there's a growing number in other countries. If regulation were more attractive and open to international capi-tal, Continental and peripheral Europe would be favourable destinations because of their modern cities and suitable infra-structure. However, regulations are extremely strict, losing the chance to attract capital and be another London or Singapore.

Normally, the candidates hired come from the big universi-ties: Harvard, Stanford, Oxford and others. Don't think, however, that you can only get into this world by paying enormous university tuition fees. There are many managers who studied at non-Ivy League universities or even didn't go to university at all. Don't think that university is a guarantee or an impediment to anything.

If a young person wants to enter this world, the most logical degree to choose is economics, although it is neither a sure bet nor the ideal degree. Any degree can work (in the City there are architects as well as graduates in art and philosophy), as long as you accompany it with an MBA and, for example, become a CFA (certified financial analyst) or a CIIA (certified international investment analyst).

When looking for talent for a fund, the great majority of selections are not made directly but via head-hunters. The best thing is to get in contact with these, or agencies specialising in the financial industry. They will guide the candidate to where there is demand. The competition for finding talent, despite the crisis, is fierce, and the search for talent never stops. They are usually looking for people with experience, with a good track record of profits and low volatility who know how to manage big portfolios and with a very specific personality profile: can handle pressure, has a passion for the market and works tirelessly. It's a good idea to generate a profit track record that includes all kinds of variables: volatility, relative share of long and shorts, maximum losses, maximum daily profits, etc.

Getting into a fund as a manager is very hard. You have to create a track record, have access to enough entry capital to ensure a solid base and look for opportunities wherever they may be.

My final suggestion for any candidate or young university student, man or woman, who wants to enter this world is to persevere, learn from all your experiences and never try to find shortcuts or rule out any type of training. You should question everything you're told. I went from seeing the economy from a neo-classical perspective to embracing the Austrian School of economics, from taking "peak oil" for granted to verifying its errors. Along the road, I have made and still make mistakes every day in many investment decisions. The key is to learn and discuss with everybody, both those you agree with and especially those you don't (provided that they are intelligent, well-informed people with interesting points of view). Don't confuse dogma and forcefulness with knowledge and authority.

If entering this world is truly your primary objective and you want to do so with all your heart, you will. You can be sure of it.

CHAPTER THIRTY-EIGHT

FAREWELL

The day I finished writing this book, I found out that a good friend of mine, Chris, with whom I had worked for years, had been fired. Chris was a big name in the hedge fund world.

We met to have a drink and eat some sushi. There weren't a lot of people at the bar, and we could talk. I recognised some familiar faces: fund managers, analysts, bankers, a model, some musicians, a fashion designer... Everybody seemed to have considered last year forgotten and was ready start from scratch on the second day of January.

I found Chris in good spirits. After 15 years in the City, he was used to good and bad times.

While he was explaining to me that he was so tired of this type of work that he was planning on possibly quitting the market, maybe joining an industrial company, travelling the world to clear his head or giving classes, a head-hunter, Herbert, approached us. My friend told him about his situation, and Herbert asked him to call him the next day because he had a couple of possibilities that might interest him. Thanking him for his friendliness, Chris told him that he wasn't sure, that he was fed up with it all and would like a change.

"Of course," Herbert answered. Then he said goodbye.

On the way home, the radio was commenting on the latest economic news. The president of the Federal Reserve, Janet Yellen, was announcing that the economy was continuing to show signs of weakness, and that she would not rule out a continuation of the stimulus programme. In Europe, signs of recovery were modest but unemployment remained stubbornly high, the European Central Bank was announcing a possible new stimulus and the United Kingdom was considering raising interest rates to combat a heated housing market. Japan was preparing more stimulus while emerging markets were starting to show weakness. Inflation in the OECD countries continued to be "moderate" in official figures, while real indicators seemed above government statistics.

Still, the press, banks, politicians, unions, citizens and financial operators were calling for more monetary expansion. Despite the daily messages from central banks, the speed of money circulation continued to fall. Economic activity was not recovering as expected.

A friend reminded me of an episode in financial history: between 1790 and 1793, 3.5 billion bills known as "assignats" were issued in France, which quickly lost 95% of their initial value. The recently appointed Minister of Finance, Clavière, promised to force the machines to print more money. Prices relentlessly continued to climb. Taxes increased and the confiscation of property accelerated. The Jacobins introduced the "Law of the Maximum", prohibiting rising prices while at the same time punishing people who refused to pay with paper money by imposing fines, jail and even the guillotine. In the end, they only managed to close shops. Finally, the riots and revolts over bread shortages finished off the French Revolution.

Needless to say, prices of speculative assets rose.

The following day, I saw the moves in prices of risky assets. The markets, along with commodities and gold, were rising. Meanwhile, the IMF moderated its global growth estimates, company earnings fluctuated between hits and misses, taxes were going up and industrial production was weak.

After a couple of weeks, Chris sent me a message through Bloomberg. The message said: "I'm back! Man, I love this game."

London, May 2014

Euro-crisis and "exceptions"

Cyprus: Another "exceptional" episode in the European crisis

> *For a small, open economy like Cyprus, euro adoption provides protection from international financial turmoil.*
>
> Jean-Claude Trichet

During the first months of 2013, news reports of the end of the crisis were constant, almost monotonous. The markets had rebounded aggressively, thanks to the words of Mario Draghi, president of the European Central Bank, who in July stated categorically that we will "do whatever it takes".

Unfortunately, the pledges of unconditional support by central banks are aimed at creating calm and gaining time but never at tackling and resolving problems.

Yet again, with the markets on the rise we forget – as always – about the problems, the deeply indebted states and oversized and fragile banking system, which have yet to be resolved.

Problem one: in 2012, the eurozone countries saw their public debt soar to 90% of their GDP. Debt-to-GDP rose 3.2 points in the single-currency countries and 4.4 points in the "Twenty-Seven". Compared with the third quarter of 2011, 22 member states increased their government debt ratio and only five reduced it. Draghi's statements inadvertently put the brakes on reform in much of Europe.

Problem two: meanwhile, the frequently announced recapitalisation of the European banks was not undertaken. Plans to slash financial sector debt by more than €1.2 trillion were shelved after a reduction of less than 30%, according to BNP, and the announcement of the regulatory framework for Basel III banks was immediately interpreted as a new episode of an "easing" of the required capitalisation conditions.

Why? Very simple. European states make use of an over-expanded financial sector to "place" a large amount of their sovereign debt. According to the ECB, as of 2013 Spanish banks accumulated almost 32% of sovereign debt, and almost 23% in the eurozone. This symbiosis has resulted in the following:

- States have not reduced their deficits and continue to get into scandalous debt.
- The state continues to monopolise available credit, thus ruining business and families.
- Banks see this as a way of generating some margin and, incidentally, of ensuring a rescue package if things get bad at the same time.
- The snowball effect of the banking problem and the vicious circle of the sovereign and financial sector debt continues to get bigger.

Ireland has been the one exception. Portugal, Greece and Belgium's Dexia were also called "isolated incidents". The bailout of Spanish banks was likewise "unique" and a "one-off".

In September 2012, an imminent bailout of Cyprus loomed. Meanwhile, there was talk of a possible bailout of Slovenia, estimated at €4 billion, which could amount to 10 or 15% of its GDP and would skyrocket its debt from an enviable 48% to 70% above GDP. However, both countries commented: "We will not need the bailout."

But, in March 2013, Cyprus took the plunge. Like all black swans, as happened to Greece, the damage done is always mistakenly perceived as "minor".

Cyprus' crisis had been brewing since the Greek bailout. A tiny country with a huge banking problem… where the financial sector exceeds 800% of GDP and a gaping hole stems from the collapse of Greek sovereign debt. Suddenly, the world was shaken from its dreams of "recovery". The event drove home the huge burden of the European banks and, above all, the contagion effect on the others if a default on government debt takes place.

Indeed, according to the Eurogroup, most deposits in Cyprus were invested "very conservatively" in Greek debt. When the cuts were applied to these bonds, the shortfall, which according to many analyses surpassed €10 billion in the balance sheets of the Cypriot banks, could not be covered. But EU regulators not only disregarded this problem: they deemed it irrelevant. "Excellent results that dispel any doubt of a state intervention in the banks." That was how the governor of the Central Bank of Cyprus had greeted the release of the endorsed stress test, which all Cypriot banks passed with flying colours (as did Spain's bankrupt savings banks, incidentally).

Not only did the EU and the ECB know about the situation of the banking structure of Cyprus – and that of all the others – they held it up as a model of investor prudence, indicating that the deposits of the Cypriot banks "are invested conservatively in sovereign bonds" (December 2011).

When Greece took the debt haircut, Cypriot-banking investments in Greek bonds plummeted. The ECB and the EU knew what could happen: the figures had not changed significantly in two years. But Brussels used its favourite strategy. It "waited for things to clear up"... until 2013, when the alarm was sounded a few months before the maturity of a large portion of Cyprus bonds.

As you know, I'm not a supporter of bailouts, although let's not forget that Cyprus helped to bail out Ireland's, Greece's, Portugal's and Spain's banks.

One of the main headaches of the European "bank restructuring" process, as Lior Jassur of HSBC reminds us, is that the priority principle of the debt haircut has been abandoned. In other words, there is no clarity as to who has priority to collect in an event of this type: bondholders, shareholders or depositors. In each case, the ECB and the EU seem to look at "where most of the money is" and change the rules in order to withdraw funds from where there is more, not from where they lawfully should.

In the case of Cyprus, the money was in bank deposits. Hence, it was necessary to use the pretext that it was a tax haven and that the money belonged to evil Russians, and with this a precedent was set.

The solution was to point the finger at "Russian mafiosi", when foreign money accounted for less than €22 billion of the almost €70 billion deposited in Cypriot banks.

All these deposits, moreover, had been audited, supervised and analysed... but the EU suddenly made the surprising announcement that Cyprus was a "tax haven" (as opposed to the "tax hell" in which we live, I imagine). Had the EU just found this out? Cyprus joined the eurozone in 2008, with a model approved and supervised by the ECB and the European authorities. Was Cyprus an evil tax haven, whereas Luxemburg was not? And what if the EU decided to claim that the bank deposits in Spain were monopolised by the informal economy or in France by "African oil oligarchs"?

Cyprus did not want to recognise the impact of the Greek government's debt hole in its banks, because by doing so it would have exposed the high risk involved in the financial sector's strategy of giving high yields to deposits which were invested in risky Greek sovereign bonds Of course, some days passed before EU leaders confirmed that deposits of less than €100,000 would be guaranteed, meaning that the rescue package would be paid for by the "wealthy", who had larger sums of money on deposit than basic rate taxpayers did.

It was dangerous to draw this distinction for one fundamental reason: the deposits of more than €100,000 had stopped the capital flight occurring in periphery banks until September 2012 – a positive trend that could be reversed when faced with the uncertainty of possible confiscatory actions.

But something was achieved. The saver, whoever he or she may be, was demonised. It is estimated that depositors holding more than €100,000 in the main Cypriot banks lost up to 65% of their money. All because the authorities failed to recognise the capitalisation problem of the banks owing to the Greek haircut and implement the capital increases that, according to any normal analysis, were needed. They preferred to hide the problem by "passing" the stress tests and easing the Basel III conditions... And the savers paid the price.

Let's not forget that, besides confiscating deposits, Cyprus has put in place capital controls that stop people taking more than a minimum amount of money out of the country. Furthermore, the EU has imposed tax rises, cuts to pensions and additional adjustments. As a result, it's estimated that the 2013/14 GDP of Cyprus will fall by between 12 and 15%. The citizens of Cyprus, in the meantime, have been cheated and trampled upon.

The contagion effect

> *Malta and Luxemburg cannot be likened to*
> *Cyprus, according to Malta and Luxembourg.*
>
> The Guardian

The risk of contagion in the rest of Europe seemed to have been checked until Jeroen Dijsselbloem, member of the Dutch Labour Party, president of the Eurogroup and of the ESM (European Stability Mechanism) had the gall to say, "Cyprus would be the template for future [European] banking crises", and that deposits of over €100,000 could not be guaranteed.

The "Dijsselbloem effect", also ironically known in the markets as "DJ Boom", "Dijsellblunder" or "DijsSellShort", caused an immediate fall in the European markets and banking sectors.

The problem is that he spoke the truth, but he did so after years of the EU hiding it. Instead of putting in place the processes for banks to receive capital injections in an orderly manner, the rules were changed to "ease" conditions and "wait for the markets to rally".

Some claim that the steps taken in Cyprus were similar to those which advocates of "bail-in" (internal rescue measures) were demanding. No. We have long been asking for capital injections – the relevant conversion of debt into shares – rather than last-minute, off-the-cuff measures, such as confiscating deposits that lead to banking panic, savers withdrawing their money and economic depression.

As president of the ESM, Dijsselbloem knew there was no money to halt a domino effect of banking bailouts like the one that could happen in Europe if (after Cyprus) Slovenia, Malta, Luxembourg or, God forbid, Italy or Spain followed suit. So Dijsselbloem decided to break with diplomatic convention with a warning that there was no money to shore up banks which don't use market mechanisms to tackle their problems and wait to be bailed out by the governments that feed them.

We are told that banking union is the solution, but we cannot create another gigantic "big bad" European bank filled with toxic assets amounting to tens of billions of euros and indebted 20 or 30 times over, as some would wish. Setting up the mechanisms of a union of hypertrophied banks is not the solution, because adding to and then hiding the risk inherent in poorly capitalised entities does not create confidence. Spain should know as much, after the "success" of the FROB (the fund for re-structuring banks that was used to promote mergers between savings banks in difficulties to give the impression of strength).

It magnifies rather than reduces the risk of accumulation. And the systemic risk permeates the whole economy. All European countries have the same problem. They accumulate sovereign debt in oversized banks with outstanding loans to zombie companies. A highly pertinent problem that can be summed up by the following points:

• The European financial sector is dangerously over-reliant on state debt being "secure".
• Almost no financial sector in the European Union will survive a haircut of its country's sovereign debt. The fallout for businesses and citizens would be enormous.
• Sovereign debt keeps growing in almost all the member states.
• The risk-containment mechanisms and access to the ECB cannot become a habit. They must be exceptional.
• European banks should have reduced their aggressive debt accumulation more than six years ago.

If it is well managed, investors should not fear an internal bailout of zombie banks. We have seen in the cases of Amagerbanken (2011) and Fjordbank Mors (2011) that the deposits of over €100,000 were subjected to minimum reductions.

In order to avoid risks, European banks must raise capital, disinvest and detach themselves from sovereign debt while they still can. They must clean up their balance sheets.

The European Central Bank's capacity to prop up a European Union where everyone is seeking to force a bailout is not limitless, even though Mario Draghi pays lip service to the idea. He knows this – that's why he's carefully holding on to his cards. The system is so delicate that the words of a European leader can create shock waves.

Dijsselbloem is not the disease. He's a symptom of an interventionist Europe, sick and improvised, where arrogance and ignorance converge when addressing financial problems. Dijsselbloem said too much, but he didn't lie. The mistake is to try to maintain this vicious circle of debt and interventionism. Because the consequences are unforeseeable.

What may happen in Spain?

Spain is different from Cyprus because it doesn't have so sizeable a volume of bank deposits held by foreigners. True. Of the €1.5 trillion held in deposits, most are held by Spanish nationals, half of them are below €100,000 (some 35,000 according to the Bank of Spain). Spain is different because the balance sheets of the banks account for three times Spain's GDP and nearly eight times that of Cyprus. Furthermore, Spain has a cushion of €60 billion from the 2012 rescue package that has not been used yet. True. But more than three times its GDP doesn't earn it an award. It's huge.

However, could Spain be different because its banks would not suffer the destruction that Cyprus has done with Greek bonds, were it forced to take a haircut in sovereign debt? Unfortunately, this is not the case. Spanish banks have accumulated more than €200 billion in sovereign debt. And if one day they do have to take a haircut, the hole would create a domino effect.

Focusing on Spain, if the Bank of Spain estimates 27% unemployment and a 1.5% fall in GDP in 2013, then the default rate and loan losses of the banking sector are underestimated. If to this, we add the fact that we have already seen an upward revision of the deficit in 2012 (which was increased from the announced 6.7% to 6.98% of the GDP, excluding bank subsidies) and that the deficit in 2013 is expected to again be 6%, we have all the ingredients for a weakened banking sector and a state having to hoard all the credit available.

So Spain and the peripheral countries need to pay close attention to their public accounts, to the deficit and to mounting public debt in order not to be another "exceptional case".

While the risk of contagion seems extremely remote, if you wish to protect your savings against similar events, the best way to do so is by investing in funds, preferably located abroad, or in gold – not futures – and non-European corporate bonds. Unfortunately, in the unlikely event that bank accounts were frozen, the stock markets of the affected country would collapse, not only because of the impact on the banking sector but also because of additional, highly contractive measures. Therefore, avoiding country risk is intrinsic to the decision to preserve capital. Investment is, of course, about taking risks, and no measure will guarantee the preservation of capital.

In Cyprus, the policy of "hide and dig in", like an ostrich waiting for everything to go away, was successful in that only 30% of the European Union member states have requested some kind of bailout or rescue package: an unprecedented "success" for a massively indebted economic system where governments tried to convince investors to accept retroactive changes to the legal framework.

The Boston Consulting Group released a report in 2011 called *Back To Mesopotamia: The Looming Threat of Debt Restructuring*, in which it warned of the risk of bank freezes and currency controls and the temptation of European countries to confiscate 11 to 15% of bank deposits, the €6.1 trillion needed to cover the risk of excessive debt in the balance sheets of their financial organisations.

However, to attack savers by confiscating their deposits is not the solution, for it would lead to a collapse of the banks for decades. It's the other way round. A regulatory environment and legal certainty are necessary to make investment attractive again – to convert bank debt into shares in an orderly but disciplined and constant fashion, and make it look like a good investment rather than a risk.

It's tough: this cannot be done in a few days, and it comes with a price tag. But it's much less harsh than ending up with freezing banks accounts, huge economic contraction and systemic risk.

Recommended Reading

Ahamed, Liaquat, *Lords of Finance: 1929, The Great Depression, and the Bankers who Broke the World*, Penguin, 2009.

Calhoun, Jack, *12 Investment Myths: Why Individual Investors are Failing Miserably and How You Can Avoid Being One of Them*, Robert D. Reed, 2011.

Cooper, George, *The Origin of Financial Crises: Central Banks, Credit Bubbles and the Efficient Market Fallacy*, Harriman House, 2008.

Fabozzi, Frank J., *Bond Markets, Analysis and Strategies*, Pearson, 2006.

Fernández, Pablo, *Valoración de Empresas*, Gestión 2000, 2001.

Fisher, Philip A., *Common Stocks and Uncommon Profits*, John Wiley & Sons, Ltd, 2003.

Hayek, Friedrich, *The Constitution of Liberty*, University of Chicago Press, Chicago, 2011.

Huerta de Soto, *Jesús, La esencia de la Escuela Austriaca*, Universidad Francisco Marroquín, 2012.

Lewis, Michael, *Boomerang: Travels in the New Third World*, W. W. Norton & Company, 2011.

Lewis, Michael, *The Big Short: Inside the Doomsday Machine*, W. W. Norton & Company, 2010.

Mallaby, Sebastian, *More Money than God: Hedge Funds and the Making of the New Elite*, Penguin, 2010.

Ontiveros, Emilio, *Una Nueva Época*, Galaxia, 2012.

Ontiveros, Emilio and Escolar, Ignacio, *El Rescate*, Aguilar, 2013.

Ozihel, Harding, *Financial Repression*, Frac Press, 2012.

Rallo, Juan Ramón, *Una Alternativa Liberal para Salir de la Crisis*, Deusto, Barcelona, 2012.

Reinhart, Carmen and Rogoff, Ken, *This Time Is Different: Eight Centuries of Financial Folly*, Princeton University Press, 2011.

Reinhart, Carmen and Rogoff, Ken, *A Decade of Debt*, Peterson Institute, 2011.

Schiff, Peter, *The Real Crash: America's Coming Bankruptcy*, St. Martin's Press, 2012.

Sefrin, Hersh, *Beyond Greed & Fear*, Oxford University Press, 2007.

Sorkin, Andrew Ross, *Too Big to Fail: The Inside Story of How Wall Street and Washington Fought to Save the Financial System – and Themselves*, Penguin, 2011.

Yergin, Daniel, *The Prize: The Epic Quest for Oil, Money, and Power*, Free Press, 2008.

Yergin, Daniel, *The Quest: Energy, Security, and the Remaking of the Modern World*, Penguin, 2012.

Index